The BBC at the Watershed

For Elizabeth, Caroline and Timothy

THE BBC AT THE WATERSHED

Kenneth Bloomfield

LIVERPOOL UNIVERSITY PRESS

First published 2008 by
Liverpool University Press
4 Cambridge Street
Liverpool
L69 7ZU

British Library Cataloguing-in-Publication data
A British Library CIP record is available

ISBN 978–1–84631–160–4

Edited and typeset by
Frances Hackeson Freelance Publishing Services, Brinscall, Lancs
Printed and bound by
Bell and Bain Ltd, Glasgow

Contents

Preface

I t is hardly surprising that many books have been published about
that unique national institution and treasure, the BBC. One thinks
of the painstaking and invaluable historical work of Asa Briggs; of
the books produced in relatively recent times by such protagonists as
Duke Hussey, John Birt, Greg Dyke and Will Wyatt; of the analytical
insights offered by Georgina Born or the polemical approach adopted
by Chris Horrie and Steve Clarke in *Fuzzy Monsters*.

What, then, are the reasons, other than narcissistic self-importance,
for my decision to offer the perspective and the views which follow?
I hope to offer a distinctive point of view at a particularly sensitive
time. Of the large number of men and women who have served on the
Board of the BBC I was amongst those fortunate enough to be offered
a second term. This enabled me to form judgements over a relatively
long period. It takes time to get a reliable feeling for so complex an
organisation. Too often one's term comes to an end just as one achieves
some degree of confidence in understanding systems, personalities and
events. I was, as it happens, the only Governor to serve throughout the
time from Birt's accession to the Director Generalship until the choice
of his successor, Greg Dyke. I was thus witness both to that significant
period of change and upheaval at the BBC termed 'Birtism' and to
the appointment of a most able but flawed successor about whom I
had profound misgivings. I had some conception of the problems of
heading large organisations. As Head of the Northern Ireland Civil
Service I had been professional head of a cadre of some 28,000 people,
a workforce very comparable with that of the BBC.

I served on the Board as one of the three National Governors. I was, however, determined from the start not to be seen simply as the voice of a provincial pressure-group or lobby, but as a contributor to the great and ongoing debates within the Corporation. There was at least one benefit flowing from my association with Northern Ireland; I did not belong to, nor could I readily be associated with, either of the main camps in national politics.

I was a senior civil servant in Northern Ireland at a period when the complexities of 'the Troubles' led to a number of classic encounters between government and BBC. It was on my home ground that there played out such episodes as Roy Mason's ferocious attack on BBC coverage, the controversy arising out of the Governors' decision to hold back a *Real Lives* programme and the introduction of a 'broadcasting ban' put in place – as it happens – shortly after an IRA attempt to assassinate me and my family.

I did not know, as I left the Board on completion of my second term in 1999, that I would be one of the penultimate generation of Governors; that my successor Fabian Monds would be the last National Governor for Northern Ireland before the Board was replaced by the Trust.

I write also because the BBC faces current difficulties and huge future challenges. In the medium term there is the struggle to maintain scope and standards within a constrained licence fee settlement. At the political level, expression is being given to the possibility that in the future some of the funding devoted to public service broadcasting could be diverted to other broadcasters. There are the growing challenges of channel proliferation and multi-platform delivery.

When I retired from the civil service after almost forty years, I entered on a period of my life when I was offered, and accepted, a great variety of assignments, some of them in areas of activity previously unknown to me. One of the benefits of this diversity is to glean insights transferable from one sphere to another. In 1994 the UK Health Ministers asked me to address the vexed question of the pay of dental practitioners within the NHS. My remit was to table options for change, and this I did. The current inability in many parts of the country to secure treatment under the NHS shows the extent to which ministers from different governments were unwilling to confront a hard truth. There has to be a choice between pretending to offer a universal service while not providing the means to fund it or identifying core services for which full and adequate provision can be made. In an ever more competitive future, and with resources inevitably under pressure, it seems to me that the BBC must think long and hard about those things that it can do best, that only it can do well or do at all, and leave to others services which are not central to its essential mission. What must be remembered, though, is that the BBC, as a world brand, is a huge international asset to Britain's prestige and interests.

1

ARRIVAL AND DEPARTURE

In August 1999 my eight-year term as the BBC's National Governor for Northern Ireland came to an end. I left that great national institution both enriched by my experience and apprehensive about the future. In what follows I will seek to describe the nature of that enrichment and the reasons for that apprehension.

At that time in 1999 my daughter Caroline was working in London as a litigation solicitor at Herbert Smith, and I had asked her to join me for dinner on my final visit to London as a Governor. When she met me in the lobby of the Langham Hotel, just across the street from Broadcasting House, I offered to take her over the road to show her some of the theatres in which the drama of BBC governance had been played out. We visited the empty Council Chamber, a place of solemnity and institutional gloom, around whose rectangular tables I had sat with my colleagues so many times. Portraits of former Directors General, of varying artistic merit (that is, the portraits), gazed down upon us from the walls. Some of those portrayed had left a lasting mark on the Corporation, for good or ill, but only one of the line appeared in stereo, as it were. From a forbidding portrait and a magisterial bust, the founding father of public service broadcasting and the BBC, John Reith, exuded a powerful mana. Somehow he resembled a bizarre hybrid of an Old Testament prophet and the lamented doleful Scots actor, Alastair Sim. I had found it eerie to observe, on occasions when the Board met the Broadcasting Council for Scotland, the striking physical resemblance between the Scottish Council's secretary, Mark Leishman, and his celebrated grandfather. Reith had so disapproved of his son-in-law as to be averse to uttering his name, commonly referring to him simply as 'that man'. One felt, indeed, that the ideal suitor in his eyes would have been a Viceroy of India, Nobel Prizewinner and/or holder of the Victoria Cross. Happily the agreeable Mark resembled Reith only in physiognomy.

While the Governors commonly assembled in the Council Chamber when meeting at Broadcasting House (rather than at the hideous Television Centre, the ghastly White City building or at a centre in the 'nations and regions'), it was interesting that the portrait gallery there did not display a single Governor or Chairman of the Corporation. The Chairmen (for no woman had held the position) were economically immortalised in photographic rather than portrait form, and their images relegated to a more modest committee room in which bodies like the Audit Committee would meet.

That evening the great building was very quiet and at first we encountered no one. I suggested to Caroline that we should take a brief look at the august floor on which the Director General, John Birt, led the management of the BBC. At that very moment Colin Browne, the Corporation's Director of Corporate Affairs, a former Director of Corporate Relations at BT and a fellow Ulsterman, appeared. I introduced Caroline, at which Colin said: 'Some of us are in John's room watching the football. So why don't you bring your daughter in to say hello?' When I made the usual noises about not wanting to intrude, Colin insisted we must come in for a moment. Like just about everyone in Britain by this time Caroline was more than familiar with the popular portrayal of Birt as a charmless, authoritarian control-freak, the sort of person beside whom Gordon Brown would appear the model of perfect bonhomie. In reality, as I shall hope to show, John was a complex and gifted man of changing moods, often introverted and shy to the point of coldness, but that evening, seated with close associates watching the football on BBC Television, he was the soul of affability. Since I was the only Governor to sit on the BBC Board from Birt's accession to the Director Generalship until the choice of Greg Dyke as his successor, I shall have much to say about Birt's influence and legacy.

Let me, though, rewind the reel to the beginning. When I was born in 1931 public service broadcasting and its instrument the British Broadcasting Corporation were still comparatively in their infancy.

Although Reith had been appointed to head the British Broadcasting Company Ltd in 1922, the public corporation subsequently known universally as the BBC had only been in existence for four years when I first became conscious of 'sounds and sweet airs' entering my infant cot. Indeed my arrival on the scene preceded the introduction of British television even in its experimental form, with a limited British Television Service operating for the first time in 1936. Only three years later the relatively few television screens darkened for the duration of the war, and a television service was not renewed until 1946. Even then, for most of us television seemed an extravagant luxury to be enjoyed only by an affluent minority.

As I grew up in suburban Belfast, BBC equated to 'the wireless'. True, the enthusiast could tune in to exotic stations in foreign parts or to Radio Luxembourg broadcasting in English, but the days of pirate radio from offshore ships or derelict wartime marine forts, let alone a whole burgeoning industry of commercial radio, lay in the hazy future.

Yet even in those early and innocent 'radio days', to plagiarise Garrison Keillor, we could begin to discern the replacement of one culture by another. From the decorous days of Jane Austen, with young ladies undertaking intricate needlework or singing duets at the piano with eligible young men, to the merry-making of Victorian or Edwardian England, families at home had provided their own active entertainment. This could be solitary or collective, and relieved by occasional visits outside the home to concerts, theatres, music halls or pubs, but with the universality of radio we had a significant shift from the active to the passive. There had, of course, already been the gramophone or phonograph and the developing cinema, but now a rich miscellany of speech, drama, music and varied news and information and entertainment was readily available in every home.

Today, when we have hundreds of radio and television channels and multiple means of delivering them, the obsessive can pursue a single dominant passion. The sports fanatic need not be diverted by other topics or themes; the golf maniac can draw upon an endless supply of golfing advice and world-wide tournament play.

The very word 'broadcasting' is worth a degree of exegetical analysis.

It can represent the capacity of radio and television to reach audiences far and wide. Yet it can also represent – and did indeed represent in the mind and vision of Reith – an opportunity to introduce to these mass audiences the unfamiliar as well as the familiar; to surprise as well as to serve them; to inform, educate and entertain. The hope was that the listener drawn (say) by the lure of the jazz band would 'stay tuned' as the schedule switched to a talk by Louis MacNeice or a performance of Elgar or Holst.

In our own modest semi-detached house in East Belfast our small family would gather of an evening around what we still termed 'the wireless'. The little window of our Philco set would take on a hospitable amber glow as we 'tuned in'. The bulky arrival of the *Boys' Own Paper* would sometimes disclose exciting diagrams showing how an amateur might assemble in a cigar box his own 'crystal set'. We were still, when all was said and done, relatively close to the pioneer days of 2LO. From very early days the BBC had established a strong regional presence, using at its Belfast 'station' talents of the dimension of Tyrone Guthrie.

The outbreak of the Second World War in 1939, when I was eight years of age, changed many things in broadcasting, as elsewhere. The suspension of the rudimentary television service made relatively little impact, but a whole population avid for news looked more and more to BBC Radio as its window on a worrying world. Even as a young boy at primary school in provincial Belfast, the gravity of Chamberlain's melancholy declaration that 'a state of war now exists' registered clearly with me. Later, returning from my first night under canvas as a Wolf Cub, I would hear the news of the German invasion of the Soviet Union.

At last, by this astonishing medium, our national leaders could speak directly and in real time to the mass of the people. Poor stammering King George VI, forcing his words out with such obvious effort, would nevertheless convey an impression of moral decency and quiet purpose. And then we had 'Winnie', Winston Churchill, with his inimitable rhetoric and growl of defiance. Much later, when we could see on television the Berlin Wall come tumbling down and the Iron Curtain being rent asunder, I was to reflect that we were the first generation in history to witness such a turning-point with our own eyes, something inconceivable in 1798 or 1848 or the days when the news of victory at Trafalgar and the death of Nelson made its slow way back to England. Churchill's wartime broadcasts to the people created a new bond between a beleaguered population and its leader, and none of this would have been possible without BBC Radio. As the war dragged on, every schoolboy became a geographer and military strategist; Tobruk and Bardia, Narvik and Surabaya moved from the fringes to our communal front door.

Of course the morale of the nation could not be sustained by inspiring rhetoric alone. No words of defiance, however eloquent, could drown the horrid news of the retreat from Dunkirk, the surrender of Singapore or the awful vulnerability of our capital ships to air attack. Unlit streets were gloomy and sinister, air raid shelters smelled of dogs' urine or worse, and the rationed diet sustained life but allowed few gastronomic pleasures. I suspect that the cynical modern listener, if exposed today to the banter of Tommy Handley and *ITMA*, would find it banal to the point of embarrassment. Yet the catchphrases of this stunningly successful programme – 'This is Funf speaking' or 'Can I do you now, sir?' – were in their own way vital ingredients in the cement holding the country together through very hard times.

Instead of access to i-Pods or mobile phones, children of my generation had *Children's Hour*, presented both nationally and locally by Uncle This or Auntie That. In our local BBC Northern Ireland version we would listen to 'Auntie Cicely', the inimitable Cicely Matthews. She encouraged children to try out their thespian skills on 'I want to be an actor', and already an enthusiastic member of the Debating Society at 'Inst.', my Belfast grammar school, I tossed my hat into this ring. So in the 1940s I entered for the first time Broadcasting House in Belfast, architecturally a sort of little brother of Portland Place, in which I would years later spend so much time. I was fascinated to see all the impedimenta of contemporary radio theatre; strange doors with no room on either side, or coconut shells to simulate galloping horses at Balaclava or the Boyne. My audition was sufficiently encouraging to lead to a small part in a broadcast radio play, alongside well-known local actors and a school contemporary in Derek Bailey, later to be a very distinguished film-maker in the sphere of opera and ballet. I was not, however, talent-spotted as the next Gielgud or Olivier; my numerous later radio and television appearances were in the area of fact rather than fiction; but I still remember the singular thrill of seeing my name in the *Radio Times*, and have retained the yellowing cutting to this day.

I was to owe a further debt to the BBC of the 1940s. As I made my way through school and towards university, I saw a need to widen my knowledge of the world, its politics, economics and culture, well beyond the boundaries of the school and examination curriculum of the day. I found no better instrument for that purpose than regular subscriptions to *The Listener*, the BBC magazine which in those days provided a permanent record of the fascinating talks given on radio by an extraordinary range of distinguished people. As I 'swotted' in the cramped little box-room I used as a study, accumulated copies of *The Listener* rose beside me like stalagmites. Long before the BBC became a partner in the Wilson government's great educational initiative, *The Listener* was for many of us a kind of open university. When, some years later, I entered the Open Competition for the Administrative Class of the Civil Service, I was pleased and astonished to find that I had scored higher marks in the so-called 'Present Day' paper (calling for wide knowledge of the contemporary world) than any other successful candidate. I felt that I owed chiefly to *The Listener* my ability to keep in touch with a wider world from a provincial backwater.

When I went up to an austere post-war Oxford in 1949 it was not to mix with the gilded youth of the Bullingdon Club from Christ Church or Magdalen but to enjoy the modest *ambiance* and predominantly grammar school ethos of what was then St Peter's Hall (now St Peter's College, of which I am an Honorary Fellow). The founding father of the Hall, Francis James Chavasse, the evangelical Bishop of Liverpool, had set out to make an Oxford education available to men of modest means. A few of my contemporaries there were exotic (one a relative of Haile Selassie, Emperor of Abyssinia), many were worthy but unexciting, but two stood out from the student body as people of extraordinary intelligence. One, John Delafons, took a distinguished First in English, rose to the rank of Deputy Secretary at the Department of the Environment, and while there won the very rare accolade (for a civil servant) of being highly praised by Richard Crossman in his discursive and controversial memoirs. The other was Colin Shaw from Liverpool College; St Peter's, for obvious reasons, maintaining close links with that city. Colin was at the heart of the college's intellectual and cultural life; producing plays, writing witty sketches for undergraduate reviews, and contributing to *Cross Keys*, the college magazine, virtually everything of distinction to appear in it.

In later days, when my daughter followed me to the college, all undergraduates aspired to become partners in City law firms or wheeler-dealers in merchant banks. In the early 1950s many of the cleverest graduates looked to the Diplomatic Service or the BBC for a prestigious and absorbing career. While John opted for the Home Civil Service, Colin joined the BBC as a producer of radio drama for the Northern Region in 1953. He was to rise steadily through the Corporation hierarchy, reaching in 1969 the highly influential position of Secretary, the vital link between Governors and management. His performance in that role would be recognised by his unprecedented designation as Chief Secretary in 1972. It seemed not inconceivable that he would in time become Director General. However, in 1976 Colin left the BBC to become Director of Television at the Independent Broadcasting Authority (IBA). There, too, he might well have expected to become Chief Executive, but from 1983 on he became heavily involved in the academic world of media and communications. It was a coincidence, then, that two contemporaries at this rather modest and obscure college should in time play important, although very different, roles in the governance of the BBC.

When I left Oxford to work in what seemed, in those innocent days, to be the quiet backwater of the Northern Ireland Civil Service, I did not envisage any future substantial involvement with the BBC other than as one of its multitude of viewers and listeners. I continued to live at home with my parents, who joined innumerable others in acquiring at last a television set (black and white of course) to view the Coronation. Neighbours from set-less homes came in, I remember, as we watched spellbound for hours the ancient and symbolic rituals of enthronement. The age of cynicism had yet to dawn. The sight of elderly gentlemen tottering backwards while bearing white wands or other courtly paraphernalia inspired curiosity and pride rather than a sense of the faintly ridiculous. 'There's Winston Churchill', we would say. 'There's Alexander.' 'That's the Duke of Norfolk, Earl Marshal of England.' (Today, I fear, many would suppose Earl Marshal to be the name of a Deputy Sheriff from Montgomery, Alabama.) Over time I have come to reflect more and more on the words given by William Shakespeare to King Henry IV:

> Thus did I keep my person fresh and new;
> My person, like a robe pontifical,
> Ne'er seen but wondered at; and so my state,
> Seldom but sumptuous, show'd like a feast,
> And won by rareness such solemnity.

His predecessor, on the other hand:

> Enfeoff'd himself to popularity;
> That, being daily swallow'd by mens' eyes,
> They surfeited with honey and began
> To loathe the taste of sweetness, whereof a little
> More than a little is by much too much.

In later years, with every royal move followed by the media, I sometimes reflected that a historic mystery too often revealed ceases to be a mystery.

It would be 1960 before I myself would appear for the first time on television. I had been appointed to pursue in North America Ulster's quest for inward industrial investment, and this appointment, coupled with my comparative youth (I was 28) attracted some local media interest at the time. Television experience gained at home was to prove useful preparation for my duties in the United States. My work over the next three years would take me all over that huge and fascinating country, from the border with Canada to the frontier with Mexico; from the Atlantic to the Pacific; to Chicago, Los Angeles, Boston, Pittsburgh, Cleveland and innumerable other industrial centres in many different states of the Union.

Alongside the powerful country-wide broadcasting systems such as CBS or NBC, there was an enormous complex of local radio and television stations, often 'network affiliates'. I had not then read Garrison

Keillor's wonderful *Radio Days* about the growth from a local diner of radio station WLT ('with lettuce and tomato'). There public service radio or television operated only at the margins of the media system. Not surprisingly in a nation dedicated to commerce ('the pursuit of life, liberty and the fast buck') the broadcasting media were driven by commercial considerations and funded by advertising revenue or sponsorship. Of course by now commercial television back home provided a serious rival to the BBC, and the programme companies were proving capable of producing programmes of high quality not only in entertainment but in other genres. Yet comparison of the competing systems convinced me of what a luxury it was to enjoy a programme uninterrupted by advertising breaks. In American radio or television studios I would encounter this irritation at its most crass. I could tolerate being addressed by the wrong name ('Welcome to Hicksville, Mr Greenfield') because what mattered was my message and not my name. But I never quite reconciled myself to the awkward hiatus in the midst of dialogue. Poised to answer some obscure and polysyllabic question: 'What, Mr Greenfield, would you identify as the paramount factors influencing a prospective industrial investor in evaluating multiple-choice opportunities?', I would be cut off on the point of replying by some such message as 'Why tolerate the discomfort of unnecessary constipation? Pasteurised Wheaties will guarantee to keep you wholesome and regular. And now back to Mr Kenneth Greenfield, who will tell us about opportunities for US investment in Western Europe.'

There was also the alarming hazard that a visiting foreigner enjoying (as I did) consular status would sometimes be expected, in some state remote from Washington or New York, to speak on behalf of his country and government on all sorts of issues quite outside his remit or brief. If one was tempted to comment unwisely on some such issue as the Queen's relationship with the Prime Minister of the day, one's response might well travel no further than the small provincial area covered by the local station. On the other hand, some busy and acute 'stringer' might pass one's unwise remarks on to a major network with the probability of attracting embarrassing attention 'back home'. Happily, although I trembled on the edge of such a pit several times, I never tumbled into it.

It was, though, a country where you had to be ready to think on your feet. In those days before Diplomatic Service retrenchments, Britain still maintained a Consul in Denver, Colorado, the 'mile-high city'. I came to know the incumbent, a lady member of the Diplomatic Service called Nancy Clay. On her first day at her new post, she had received a welcoming phone call from a local State Senator. 'Why don't you come on down to the State Capitol and meet some folks?' When Nancy entered the impressive legislative building, her host said: 'Let's go into the Chamber now.' 'Are you quite sure,' she asked, 'that's all right?' 'Yeah, sure. Come on in with me.' So in strode Nancy Clay, to hear from the chair the amazing declaration, 'We welcome today the Honorable Nancy Clay, who will deliver a personal message from Her Majesty the Queen.' An unnerving test; but passed, I am sure, with flying colours.

Or again, I was invited to a lunch meeting at the Economic Club of Detroit. There I was, a green young man on the cusp of 30, enjoying the middle-ranking status of a Consul or First Secretary, when a friendly American invited me to 'come over and meet some folks'. These 'folks' proved to be the current chief executives of General Motors, Ford and Chrysler, and I struggled to respond to such questions as: 'And how is the dear Chancellor of the Exchequer?'

Towards the end of our term in North America my young wife Elizabeth encountered another facet of American broadcasting. Today 'game shows' of one sort or another occupy television screens around the world. At that time, in 1963, the primary show of this genre, screened across America and watched by audiences of many millions, was *The Price is Right*, moderated by one Bill Cullen. The rules of the game were fatuously simple. Objects of some value would be exhibited to the mass audience and to a chosen panel in the NBC studio at Rockefeller Centre in New York. Panel members had to guess the hidden value of the prize, which would be won by the contestant getting closest to the concealed value without exceeding it. Elizabeth had turned up simply to see a TV show being made, but unexpectedly was chosen to be a competitor. So unerring was her sense of value and so sharp her competitive instinct, honed on the tennis courts and elsewhere, that she topped the prize-list twice, accordingly appeared on three successive shows, and won multiple prizes including a mink coat and a grand piano. Far away in Dallas, Texas, an Ulster émigré phoned his mother in Belfast. 'Unless I'm mistaken, I've just seen Elizabeth Ramsey [my wife's maiden name] on the TV ...'

One distinct impression I have retained from those years is of the articulate self-confidence of the average American, even those of school or college age. How often, in Britain, do we see some couple interviewed about a family triumph or disaster. Father normally keeps his mouth shut; mother offers a few diffident words. On American news programmes one can see rich and poor, young and old, black and white prepared to offer their views with confidence and eloquence.

If interviewees are loquacious, interviewers can verge on the garrulous. In the early 1960s Dave Garroway's *Today* show was presented by the Robin Day or Jeremy Paxman of American television. Only once did I see Garroway's loquacity totally stymied. His morning guest was Clement Attlee, then in retirement but famous even when serving as Prime Minister for his economy of speech. 'Why do I have to leave the Government, Prime Minister?' 'No good. Got to go.' Or to Professor Harold Laski: 'A period of silence from you would be appreciated.' In typical fashion Garroway posed for the elderly statesman a series of long, circumlocutory questions, loaded with subordinate clauses. 'And so, Earl Attlee, having regard to the emerging geo-political factors in the world today, would you say, balancing one consideration with another, that in all probability the counter-intuitive influences that ... blah, blah, blah ...' To which Clem, poised in his chair like an ageing but still spry sparrow, would answer 'Yes' or 'No', or if he felt the need for longer exposition 'Because I was against it.'

However in 1963 an unexpected career development was to bring me over time much closer to the broadcasting and other media. I had fully expected to serve in New York for at least four years, and might well have been tempted on completion of that term to seek a permanent future in the United States, which I had found exhilarating. My posting there had coincided with the Kennedy presidency, and however critical some later aspects of the later re-assessment of his career and person- ality, it seemed at the time a peculiarly exciting period in American life, in spite of the intense if short-lived shudders induced by the Cuban missiles crisis.

However, as I competed my third year in New York the politics of my native Northern Ireland took a new turn. Lord Brookeborough, Prime Minister for nineteen years of complacent inactivity, at last resigned to be replaced by the 48-year-old Terence O'Neill, with whom I had worked closely in the 1950s as his Private Secretary at the Ministry of Finance. The new PM telephoned me in New York to say that he wanted me to return to Belfast to serve as deputy to the Cabinet Secretary. In my time in Finance I had become, over time, and as I gained his confidence, much more a confidant than a 'bag carrier'. I decided to follow his star.

O'Neill by disposition was much more presidential than prime ministerial, and over time his tightly-knit group at Stormont Castle (the 10 Downing Street of Northern Ireland) became known – not entirely affectionately – as 'the presidential aides'. To the extent that this jest had substance, I was to be the Ted Sorenson of the Stormont 'White House', the ideas-man and word-spinner of the regime.

One could expect local media, both written and broadcast, to take a close interest in the activities of a local Prime Minister, particularly such a 'new broom' as Terence O'Neill. What we could not foresee in 1963 was that from 1966 onwards a mounting storm would blow little provincial Northern Ireland into the mainstream of national and worldwide media interest. Over time I made it my business to get to know the senior people in BBC Northern Ireland, and in particular successive Regional Controllers. There was the shrewd but affable Waldo Maguire, the 'man from the Montiaghs' (pronounced 'Munchies'), and Dick Francis, a former editor of *Panorama*. I must have spent many happy hours watching *Panorama* in its heyday. I recall in particular a programme focusing on the problems then facing British industry. In the first part of the programme we saw the formal ceremony marking the opening of a new automotive assembly line in Korea, before a company including the British George Turnbull, an expert recruited by the Koreans from the British motor industry. There was much ritual bowing before a dais or altar improbably adorned with a pig's head. The second part of the programme consisted of a panel discussion chaired by the formidable Robin Day, his face set in a characteristic frown just this side of absolute fury. As was inevitable in those times, the panel included a senior trade union figure, in this case the influential and vocal Hugh Scanlon. 'Well, Mr Scanlon,' asked Day, bringing his full invigilator's scowl to bear on the captive trade unionist, 'What are you prepared to do to promote the economic welfare of this country?' 'Almost anything, Robin,' Scanlon disarmingly replied, 'as long as I'm not expected to bow down to a pig's head.'

Dick Francis and his vivacious wife Penny were engaging and sociable. Dick had, I remember, a wonderful story from the brief Indo-Pakistan war which he had covered for the BBC. At last, with India prevailing, the rival generals encountered each other. Embarrassingly, both had been at Sandhurst in earlier days. There was a brief awkward pause before they plunged into reminiscence and exchanged impressions of the campaign.

As public order deteriorated, O'Neill would be interviewed more and more often, frequently on the steps of Stormont Castle, for local, national or foreign television. But as the storm-clouds grew ever more threatening in late 1968 the Prime Minister concluded that he ought to speak to the people at large about the nature of the growing crisis, and its implications for the future of Northern Ireland. All day long, in my modest office adjacent to the Cabinet Room, I polished and re-polished an unprecedented appeal to public opinion. Such was the pressure of time and events that I had to take a text festooned with late amendments to Broadcasting House in central Belfast and there dictate it to a BBC typist for transcription on to the long paper roll inserted into the primitive autocue of the day. On arrival at the studio, O'Neill inserted an introductory sentence drawing on an image used in an earlier speech. 'Ulster stands at the crossroads', he began, in his strange pseudo-Churchillian mode of speech, and thereafter the 'Crossroads Speech' became and probably remains the best-known single speech of any Northern Ireland Prime Minister. When the broadcast was completed, I popped the autocue roll into my pocket, and I have it still. The outcome was a fascinating and informative demonstration both of the power of television and the limits of that power. The immediate impact was a huge manifestation of support, but that support was to prove flimsy and short-lived in the face of new developments and tactical mistakes.

I recall, too, from those years, an occasion when the 'top brass' of BBC Television had indicated an interest in getting to know O'Neill better. I accompanied him to a private dinner at Television Centre, where we met Corporation mandarins like Huw Wheldon and Brian Tesler.

BBC and other media interest grew exponentially as the Northern Ireland 'Troubles' persisted and deepened. Household names began to make regular forays to Belfast and Derry. On two significant occasions in particular BBC coverage played a critical part in shifting the focus of decision-making from Belfast to London. The pictures of a British MP, Gerry Fitt, batoned and bloody as the RUC confronted a civil rights march in Derry, flushed down the plughole of history a decades-old convention of non-intervention in Northern Ireland's domestic affairs. Still more dramatic were the pictures from 'Bloody Sunday' in the same turbulent city, hastening the introduction of direct rule of the province from Westminster.

Television journalists had to cover, often at real risk to themselves, many other brutal and bloody incidents. I came to realise, though, the danger of assuming that what we saw on television always represented 'the truth, the whole truth, and nothing but the truth'. Viewers were understandably inclined to say: 'I know exactly what happened. I saw it on the box with my own eyes.' Yet the film of A attacking B may have followed hard upon the unfilmed episode of B attacking A. Nor was the analysis of famous 'visiting firemen' of the media, parachuted into the province for specific assignments, always as sensitive to underlying reality as the perception of less well-known journalists deeply rooted in the local scene and familiar with every nuance.

Moreover, in circumstances like these, competing forces use propaganda as a weapon in their struggle. The Frank Cooper who confronted the Ulster Workers' Council strike of 1974 was the same Frank Cooper who, as Permanent Secretary at the Ministry of Defence, later kept the British press on a very tight rein during the Falklands campaign. Radical revolutionary movements are very quick and adept about establishing with the minimum of delay their version of some controversial event. If lawful authority waits too long to establish and publicise the true facts, these may never penetrate the protective screen of adversarial untruth. Yet, if speed of reaction is unduly prioritised over thoroughness and reliability, lawful authority may be profoundly embarrassed, as in the case of the Gibraltar shootings in March 1988, by authorising a release which does not stand up to subsequent rigorous scrutiny. If governments are not very good at admitting they have got something wrong, it has to be said that the BBC itself has not always shown great enthusiasm for the *mea culpa*.

Another recollection from the declining days of the old Stormont system, with Brian Faulkner serving as the last Prime Minister, was the endless pressure for making him available for media questioning. I recall, for example, a long, long telephone conversation in which David Frost brought to bear all his formidable talents of persuasion and flattery to convince me that I should overcome Faulkner's resistance to participate in a long interview at that time and in those circumstances. It was by no means the case that Faulkner was a shrinking violet as far as interviews were concerned; indeed he positively enjoyed the cut and thrust, preferably with unbated weapons. Yet this request came at a time when it seemed to all of us, the Prime Minister included, that he should not foreclose any options. He did not wish to be elbowed into the position of defending traditional party stances which could prove untenable. I am afraid I lost my patience towards the end of Frost's sustained barrage. 'Mr Frost,' I declared rather pompously, 'while you are in the entertainment business, we are in the government business.'

When direct rule, under the benign leadership of William Whitelaw, was introduced in 1972, the hope of all of us was that devolution could be restored before too long on a broadly acceptable basis. On 1st January 1974 Faulkner took the brave step of leading his party, or at least that part of it remaining loyal to him, into a 'power-sharing' government alongside the moderate nationalist SDLP and the centrist, non-sectarian Alliance Party. Within a few months this fragile government was to be overthrown by the mass protest, part peaceful and part coercive, known to history as the Ulster Workers' Council strike (UWC). A critical element in the success of the strikers was the adherence to their cause of workers in the principal power stations and the consequent stranglehold over electricity supply. It goes without saying that, as the unprecedented drama played itself out, the media sought to report the course of events in great detail. BBC Northern Ireland played a significant and controversial role in reflecting, and some would say inflating, the sense of crisis. At the centre of this controversy was the crucial role of a certain Hugo Patterson, appearing as spokesman for the Northern Ireland Electricity Service (NIES). In my experience only the doleful Ministry of Defence spokesman during the Falklands War conveyed a comparable air of pervading gloom. It was as if the mounting message was: 'Their hands are round your throat ... Their grip is tightening ... Your face is going blue ... It can't be long now.' There were those in the 'bunker' at Stormont – and I was amongst them – who were profoundly irritated that a great public institution seemed to be adopting an attitude of neutrality as between a government lawfully constituted, however unpopular, and those seeking to overthrow it by measures which did not exclude coercion and intimidation. Later an experienced local broadcaster, Don Anderson, was to write an informative book about these events. Reviewing the matter in retrospect, I would be more critical of government than the BBC. Hugo Patterson was the servant of a public utility; the ultimate oversight of that undertaking lay with the Ministry of Commerce headed at ministerial level by John Hume of the SDLP, a leading member of the power-sharing Executive and vociferous opponent of the strike. He could, I would have thought, have made it clear to the management of the NIES that that no spokesman for that organisation was to be allowed to make statements bound to undermine public confidence. In the absence of such a directive, and with restrictions in electricity supply a central issue, it was naive to suppose that the BBC would fail to carry bulletins from an authoritative source. Yet this issue raised questions of fundamental importance about the role, functions and responsibilities of the BBC. As 'the national broadcaster', should the Corporation be on the side of 'our boys' even to the extent of self-censorship when coverage of controversial events could damage the national interest?

Of course in a great many jurisdictions it was taken for granted that the national broadcaster would be an instrument of state power. When, long after my retirement from the civil service but while still serving as a BBC Governor, I spent some time in Bangladesh as a consultant on civil service reform there, the local British Council invited me to speak to newspaper editors in Dacca about the Corporation and its work. At the end of my talk one of the editors present observed: 'We will always be grateful to the BBC for supporting us during our war of independence.' I felt bound to reply: 'If telling the truth about what was happening proved helpful to your cause, so be it. But we don't take sides in our own politics, and would never seek to do so in the affairs of other countries.' I shall comment later on the extent to which British politicians are comfortable with such assurances.

What was incontestable was that in many countries the state broadcaster was no more than an arm of government; and even in free societies and liberal democracies, few if any of our counterparts enjoyed the degree of independence and the security of resources to play a role in any way comparable. Over the Irish border, RTE had moved to a hybrid funding basis and a later fraternal visit to CBC in Canada left me with a depressing impression of a depleted and under-resourced organisation, whose Board did not even enjoy the power to choose their own Chief Executive.

After the collapse of the 'power-sharing' Executive I served for a number of years as a departmental Permanent Secretary, dealing in succession with the environment and the economy. However in 1984 I became, as Head of the Northern Ireland Civil Service, the principal local adviser to successive Secretaries of State: in my case Douglas Hurd, Tom King and Peter Brooke. In that earlier period between 1974 and 1984 I had two significant experiences relevant to my future role at the BBC.

In 1977 extensive preparations were being made to celebrate the Silver Jubilee of Queen Elizabeth, and plans were being made for royal visits to all parts of the United Kingdom. Inevitably the question arose; should the Queen include Northern Ireland in her Jubilee itinerary or not? That majority of the local population who remained intensely loyal to the Crown would consider it an affront, and a concession to dissidence, if Northern Ireland could not share to the full in the national celebrations. Yet the province was still in the thick of a bitter and bloody war waged by terrorist organisations utterly careless of innocent life and anxious to record spectacular strikes against the British establishment. The fear that the Queen could be exposed to danger was not fanciful. Terrorists would not have pursued an elderly retired sailor to a tranquil bay in the north-west of Ireland if he had not been associated with the Royal Family.

At that time we included amongst our close friends Tim Willis, Managing Director for Times Newspapers of the *Belfast Telegraph*, and his sociable wife Oenone. We would quite often be guests at their rural retreat amongst the drumlins of County Down. Invited to dinner one evening in early 1977, we arrived, as one often does on such occasions, to half-hear introductions against a buzz of conversation. The tall, craggy guest of honour seemed to be the Duke of Somewhere-or-other. Why, then, was his wife addressed as 'Lady Susan'? Had I overlooked some obscure change in protocol while concentrating on my departmental remit of roads and transport, housing and planning, water and sewerage? I was reminded of a similar confusion years before when we had been guests of the then GOC (Northern Ireland) at his residence Cloonagh House on the fringes of Belfast (long since demolished to make way for housing estates of impeccably republican hue). Everyone, soldier or civilian, was in black tie. My wife had not heard clearly, against the animated buzz of conversation, the name of her neighbour at table. 'Tell me who you are and what you do', she innocently asked, to which the Chief of the General Staff replied, 'I suppose I might be described as the professional head of the Army.'

So in due course it became clear at the Willis party that our principal guest was Lady Susan Hussey, a sister of the well-known Tory politician William Waldegrave, a long-standing Lady in Waiting and close personal friend of the Queen and other members of the Royal Family. In the last resort, HM would have to look to the Government, and particularly to the Secretary of State Roy Mason, for official guidance about the advisability of a Jubilee visit to Northern Ireland. Nevertheless, it appeared, she would welcome a more personal view of how such a visit might be received; and I had been invited not for my current preoccupation with reservoirs and sewage works but because of years spent in the old Cabinet Office very close indeed to the politics of Northern Ireland. Willis had organised this encounter because Lady Susan's husband, Marmaduke ('Duke' or 'Dukie') Hussey was at this time Rupert Murdoch's man as Chief Executive at Times Newspapers. I enjoyed his ebullient company that evening, but of course had no idea how our paths would cross years later, or in what context. In the event, with the encouragement of the resolute Mason, the Queen would visit both Hillsborough and Coleraine to a rousing reception.

Another occasion was less comfortable or pleasant. At the material time the National Governor of the BBC for Northern Ireland was the hotelier W. P. (Bill) O'Hara, the first Roman Catholic to hold that position. Because he and I had been friends for many years, it was sometimes assumed that I must have contrived his appointment. In truth, as a departmental Permanent Secretary I had no role whatever in such appointments at that time. No doubt it had occurred to someone in authority, whether civil servant or politician, that it was high time to break the endless succession of Protestant appointees. Bill had served for a time as a councillor in local government, but his political views were more centrist than stridently nationalist or republican. After his appointment I had met on one occasion at his home the then Vice Chairman of the BBC, Mark Bonham-Carter, a grandson of H. H. Asquith.

Since the introduction of National Governors to the Board in 1952, the appointees from Northern Ireland had for much of the time been members of the Protestant and Unionist ascendancy. Sir Henry Mulholland and Ritchie McKee had been firmly in that camp; the latter a regular golfing partner of Basil Brooke. A rather more adventurous choice was made with the appointment of Sir Richard Pim in 1963. As a former Inspector General of the RUC he could be regarded as being cast from the same mould as his predecessors. However as an RNVR Captain he had managed Winston Churchill's underground map-room and travelled with the great man to wartime conferences. He had marvellous stories of those days, some of them no doubt apocryphal. In one of these Churchill enters the map-room, the wall festooned with pins across northern Normandy soon after D-day. 'Pim, place your finger on the map of France at St Malo. Then follow Route Nationale such-and-such some 45 kilometres inland and tell me where you are.' 'I seem to be at the village of So-and-So, Prime Minister'. 'Quite right. Absolutely right. It was there we spent the first night of our honeymoon. We had roast chicken turned on a spit. Always remember, Pim, some of the greatest pleasures of this life are gastronomical.'

With his elegant appearance, soldierly bearing and quick wit, Pim was no plodding copper. Typically, when I received a CB in the Honours List, Dick Pim wrote to me (citing a famous Northern Ireland civil servant of an earlier generation) 'Duggan always used to say that the Bath is the only Honour which a gentleman could possibly accept.' And when Margaret Thatcher came to open the war-rooms to the public, Pim wrote to me that she had greeted him with a singular lack of warmth. 'Probably thinking another wet Pym, I expect.'

In 1968 Pim had been succeeded in turn by a charming eccentric aristocrat, Lord (Henry) Dunleath, whose 'place' at Ballywalter reminded one of a Victorian club, whose enthusiasms included racing fast cars and preserving venerable pipe organs, and who would nail his political colours to the mast of the moderate, centrist and non-sectarian Alliance Party. Bill O'Hara would succeed him, followed by Lady (Lucy) Faulkner, widow of Northern Ireland's last Prime Minister who had led the short-lived power-sharing Executive.

While Bill O'Hara served on the Board and Roy Mason governed from Stormont Castle as Secretary of State, the BBC Chairman of the time, Michael Swann, visited Northern Ireland and invited Mason to be guest at a dinner to be held at the Culloden Hotel, between Holywood and Bangor. Bill invited me to come to this event as his personal guest, quite unaware that he was to make me a witness to one of the most extraordinary exchanges ever to take place between government and the BBC. What happened was this. The gentlemanly academic Swann, as the serving Chairman of the BBC, welcomed Mason to the dinner, expressed his pleasure at being in Northern Ireland and asked if the Secretary of State would like to say a few words. What ensued can only be described as a thermonuclear explosion of rage and spleen. The BBC, Mason asserted, were disgracefully failing to support the security forces of our country and irresponsibly giving aid and comfort to our enemies. This diatribe could by no stretch of the imagination be viewed as a constructive contribution to a rational discussion or debate. Thereafter one of the senior people at BBC Northern Ireland, Cecil Taylor, who had long experience and good judgement, made a valiant attempt to explain and justify the BBC's role in illustrating and explaining reality, even at the risk of provoking discomfort in government. By then I would have preferred to be in a steaming jungle or an icy waste, for if my loyalty was due to the Secretary of State, my sympathy lay with the BBC. There was no real debate: there was no meeting of minds. This disastrous encounter retains a deservedly notorious place in the annals of the BBC as 'the Battle of Culloden'.

My promotion to Head of the Civil Service in 1984 necessarily brought me closer to the interface between government and the BBC. In that role I was responsible, amongst other things, for a Central Appointments Unit designed to maintain a record of those likely to be suitable for diverse public appointments. Of course broadcasting had never been a matter devolved to the Northern Ireland Cabinet or Executive while we had one, and although Governors of the BBC were appointed by the Queen in Council, she would act on the advice (at that time) of the Home Secretary as the responsible minister. In turn, though, the Home Secretary would understandably look to the Secretary of State for Northern Ireland for suggestions, and he then might well draw upon his most senior local adviser's knowledge of local personalities. There were, in fact, two vacancies in the post of National Governor during my term of office as Head; first, on the retirement of Lucy Faulkner in 1985, and later on the retirement of her successor James Kincade, envisaged as occurring in 1990.

The 1985 vacancy cropped up at a particularly delicate time. The BBC had made a *Real Lives* programme designed to show the nature of the political polarisation in Northern Ireland. They had focused on Londonderry (or Derry for those who preferred it) and on the part played in the politics of that area and Northern Ireland as a whole by Gregory Campbell of the DUP and Martin McGuinness of Sinn Fein. Margaret Thatcher, hearing of these plans on a visit to the United States, had expressed great displeasure at what she saw as a platform to be afforded to a practitioner of terrorism (bearing, it has to be said, a remarkable resemblance to the current Deputy First Minister of Northern Ireland). Taking his cue from an incensed Prime Minister, the Home Secretary, Leon Brittan, wrote to the Chairman of the BBC expressing his concern, and on receipt of this shot across their bows the Governors decided to view the programme before transmission. In doing so, they put themselves in an utterly false position. Whatever the role of the Governors might be – and as I shall explain later it was in some respects dangerously ill-defined – it did not include acting as an editor or censor of individual programmes. Their post-viewing decision to defer screening created at once the most serious breach between professional broadcasters and the Governors. Unhappily all of this was occurring while the Director General, Alasdair Milne, was out of the country. No one had a better or more balanced judgement of the BBC's responsibility to Northern Ireland than the wise and experienced Controller in Belfast, James Hawthorne, and he made it quite clear that he was appalled by the action of the Board. And indeed, when the programme, with very modest changes, was ultimately screened, life in Northern Ireland went on much as before.

Two famous schools in the city of Belfast, the Royal Belfast Academical Institution ('Inst') and the Methodist College ('Methody') are long-standing rivals on the rugby field and elsewhere. But they are friendly rivals, which at heart respect each other. I had come to know well James Kincade, the headmaster of Methody, as a highly intelligent, humane man of good judgement, and I put my Inst colours behind me when I suggested Jim as a possible successor to Lucy Faulkner, and was gratified when this suggestion found favour.

I hope I have made it clear that I believe the government of the day got it wrong at the 'Battle of Culloden' and in handling the episode of *Real Lives*. It would, however, be a mistake to suppose that BBC postures were at all times beyond reproach. During Douglas Hurd's relatively brief period as Secretary of State for Northern Ireland I found myself seated at a Hillsborough Castle dinner one evening opposite Alasdair Milne. In an entirely unaggressive and careful way I ventured the thought that media must have to be wary on occasions to avoid manipulation by extreme groups mounting 'stunts' specifically for their benefit. I knew, in fact, that the sniff of a camera in certain areas could be guaranteed to produce a showy flourishing of arms carried by hooded men to suggest their de facto control. Milne's reaction to this point, made as it was in an entirely inoffensive way, was to treat it as a head-on assault on the integrity and editorial independence of the BBC. I thought his reaction extreme, hysterical, conceited and offensive, and I was to shed no tears when learning of his later rather brutal dismissal.

Events in September 1988 were to ensure me of an unsought footnote in the history of broadcasting. This had already proved a particularly bloody year in the 'armed struggle' of the IRA. As Head of the Civil Service I enjoyed some fairly rudimentary protective measures. Windows in our house at Crawfordsburn had been replaced by reinforced glass, and while we were awake a form of CCTV system enabled us to see who had come to the front door before opening it. But there was no substantial fencing around our garden, no gate or other barrier to admission. Unlike ministers, we had no bodyguards or armoured cars in which to travel. There were, I admit, moments as I stopped my Rover at the head of our drive before turning on to the Ballymullan Road when I reflected what a 'sitting target' I would make. But I carried no personal protection and had never sought it. Perhaps naively, I felt that my widely-known association, through a programme called 'Making Belfast Work', with efforts to improve economic and social conditions in deprived areas of the city might have won me some credit even in districts dominated by republican politics. None of this dissuaded an 'active service unit' of the IRA from making its way literally to our front door in the early hours of the morning, and placing round the house what local newspapers termed a 'necklace of death', a ring of four bombs of Libyan-donated Semtex so placed around the house as to bring the whole structure down around us – my wife Elizabeth, my 18-year-old son Timothy and myself – as we slept. For whatever fortuitous reason, only two of these bombs exploded as planned. The damage they had done was in all conscience bad enough, since we lost our home and cherished possessions – books won as prizes at school, favourite pictures by local artists – but we emerged uninjured if shaken.

If this attack against an unprotected family was cowardly and disgraceful, the political comments which followed were no less contemptible. Claiming 'credit' for the attack, the Belfast Brigade of the IRA issued what was termed by a newspaper of nationalist sympathies a 'crude and gloating statement' pointing out how lucky I was that only my 'spoils of war' had been affected.

Thereafter Gerry Adams himself was interviewed about the attack on BBC Northern Ireland's current affairs programme *Newstalk*. This interview produced not one word of apology or regret. The IRA used the opportunity to describe me as 'the key administrator of British colonial policy in Northern Ireland' and to warn civil service colleagues that they should 'resign their posts or face the consequences'. For myself, I issued a statement within hours of the attack to make it clear that I would not be deterred from doing my duty and was confident that colleagues would respond in the same way.

The chronology of the next few days is significant. On 26th September the Secretary of State, Tom King, invited me to join him at a Hillsborough Castle dinner for the 'Sunday lobby', embodying journalists from the main British Sunday papers. It was inevitable that, only a fortnight after the destruction of our home, the attack would be a subject for discussion. I made our guests fully aware of my sense of outrage at this assassination attempt, inevitably compounded by the determination of the republican leadership to exploit it in a wider effort to intimidate professional colleagues.

Two days later, the Prime Minister, Mrs Thatcher, accompanied by her husband Denis, came on a pre-planned visit to Northern Ireland. Part of the programme would afford an opportunity for me and my Permanent Secretary colleagues to meet the PM. However, when Elizabeth and I arrived at Hillsborough Castle we were told that the Thatchers wished to have a private conversation with us before they joined the other guests. Thus we came to talk to them face to face in the 'Queen's bedroom' of the castle. I was not always an admirer of the harsh, domineering style of the 'Iron Lady', but of course she herself had experienced to the full at Brighton what it was like to witness brutal terrorism and to escape death by a hand's breadth. They listened most sympathetically to the account of our experiences, and were kind and supportive in the extreme. Mrs. Thatcher had already written a personal letter on the day of the attack to say 'how very much I admire the statement which you have issued. It is very courageous and I am sure will help to steady the Northern Ireland Civil Service, who do such remarkable service for the community.' Later in the week, the Cabinet, meeting for the first time since the attack, had instructed the Cabinet

Secretary Sir Robin Butler to express 'their deep appreciation of your reaction to the incident which they regarded as being in the highest traditions of the public service'.

Against this background, it was perhaps inevitable that our unhappy experience in the previous month should become linked with the decision taken on 19th October by the Home Secretary Douglas Hurd (King's predecessor as Secretary of State for Northern Ireland) to introduce the so-called 'broadcasting ban' forbidding the broad-casting media from permitting the voices of terrorist leaders to be heard on radio or television. The adage 'post hoc ergo propter hoc' largely prevailed. For example the *Mail on Sunday*, one of the papers represented at the Hillsborough Castle dinner, wrote as follows:

> A fortnight later [that is, later than the attack on our home] Sir Kenneth was at dinner with Tom King ... and visitors from London. But his deepest fury was reserved not for the IRA but for the media. Never, he said, had he been made more angry than by television and radio reports on the night of the explosion. These, with the active connivance of the broadcasters, showed the IRA in triumphant mode. He was described as 'the key administrator of British Colonial policy in Northern Ireland'. Ulster civil servants were warned that they should resign their posts or 'face the consequences'. Two days later, Mrs. Thatcher flew to Ulster where she met 12 of Ulster's senior civil servants led by Sir Kenneth. There she was asked to imagine the effect broadcasts of this kind must have on civil servants and their families. She was asked to imagine how it must be for all the thousands of relatives of those murdered in Northern Ireland having to sit in their living rooms and listen to the apologists for the IRA being treated as if they had a legitimate point of view to explain squalid and barbaric murders. Mrs. Thatcher was profoundly moved by what she heard. From that moment the days of unrestricted reporting in Northern Ireland were numbered.

Rather closer to the truth, it seems to me, was a chapter on the ban contributed by Ed Moloney, a very experienced and well-informed local journalist, to the book *The Media and Northern Ireland* edited by Bill Rolston and published in 1991. He concluded that the ban was 'brought rapidly to the fore of Mrs. Thatcher's list of measures when Gerry Adams warned government officials that they all ran the risk of attack after the IRA bombed the home of Northern Ireland's top civil servant, Sir Kenneth Bloomfield'.

What, then, was the truth of my involvement (if any) in the Government's controversial banning decision? I did not argue for this course either with the Secretary of State or the Prime Minister. Was the Government's decision nevertheless influenced by the crass IRA statements following the attack of 12th September? That is indeed possible. My own unpleasant experience was far from being the only or the worst terrorist outrage of 1988, but it may have been the final element tipping the scales. Was it self-evidently perverse? A Tory Government, seeking to be strong on law and order, did not find it easy to explain why a measure taken in the Irish Republic years before, by Conor Cruise O'Brien as the responsible minister, should not be replicated in Northern Ireland where subversive organisations represented a much greater threat.

Did I myself immediately realise that it had been a mistake? The honest answer is 'No'; I was not in a mood to be antipathetic to strong anti-terrorist measures after terrorism had come, in the most literal sense, to our own front door.

Did I, then, change my view solely on the basis of my experience as a BBC Governor? No; well within the period of almost three years remaining before I joined the BBC Board I had begun to see the outworking of the ban as counter-productive. Since every newspaper, and every non-British media outlet would continue to feature the pronouncements of the IRA/Sinn Fein leadership, broadcasting media could hardly retain credibility if appearing to be struck by total deafness. So it came about that we had the frankly farcical situation of actors pronouncing the words of Adams and others, sometimes more convincingly than the 'politicians' themselves.

Moreover, whether we liked it or not America in general and Irish-America in particular had become a powerful player in the continuing drama of Northern Ireland. The idea of media censorship, of any kind or for any reason, was anathema in the United States. After all, not many years had passed since the assiduity of reporters at the *Washington Post* had exposed the Watergate affair and its subsequent cover-up, leading to the resignation of 'the world's most powerful man'.

Another reason for growing uneasiness on my part was based

upon a misjudgement of what was likely to happen when and if the ban was lifted. One could not cross-examine an actor reading the words of Adams or another; if those words had to be delivered in person, there would be an opportunity to question, to dig beneath the smooth surface of republican rhetoric. In the event it seemed to me, after the ban was finally removed, that Adams and others batted off the questions of skilled television interviewers with surprising ease. As I listened to them, in the days before the concept of being 'on message' had been developed by the Mandelsons and the Campbells, I was strongly reminded of an aspect of my Oxford experience. St Peter's Hall, reflecting its modest endowment and evangelical tradition, was more likely to produce vicars for obscure Church of England parishes than raving radicals. Yet, improbably enough, one of my contemporaries there had been a leading member of the Communist Party in the university. It is an agreeable part of the Oxford tradition for old members of a college to be invited back at intervals for a periodic 'gaudy', or what the Americans would call a 'class reunion'. On my first such return J.T. was there. 'What are you doing now?' I asked, expecting an answer like 'working for ICI' or 'running a bank'. 'You may remember my political interests. I've still got them. I'm Youth Officer of the Party.' Years later still I would read in the college magazine that he was teaching at a university in East Berlin. Even when the rest of us were callow undergraduates questioning everything, J.T. was always 'on message'; thoroughly briefed on the approved party line. Having witnessed broadcasts like Jeremy Paxman's pursuit of Michael Howard, I had foolishly persuaded myself that the heavy hitters of the BBC would easily penetrate the armour of such as Gerry Adams. Yet I can recall only one occasion post-ban when Adams was driven conspicuously on the defensive, and this was not in dialogue with a professional broadcaster but with the local Presbyterian cleric, John Dunlop, a former Moderator of the General Assembly.

The *Real Lives* fiasco and the controversy surrounding the broadcasting ban illustrated that events in Northern Ireland had presented the BBC with a serious and continuing challenge, not just in terms of professional coverage, but in terms of underlying issues of principle. When, if at all, should Governors seek to view a programme in advance of transmission? How should it deal with the statements of people at liberty, facing no specific charge, but commonly known to represent a front for criminal and terrorist organisations?

In April 1990 I was in the last year of my civil service career, and as it happened it was Northern Ireland's 'turn' to receive one of those visits from the BBC Boards of Governors and management periodically paid to Scotland, Wales or Northern Ireland. At a suitable venue in each place the Corporation would entertain local worthies to dinner. There the Chairman of the day would deliver a 'state of the Corporation' address, with emphasis on the BBC's local involvement, while one of the invited local guests would speak for his or her community. I was not surprised to receive an invitation to attend; as the professional head of an organisation of some 28,000 people I represented an important interest in our society. I had also, which some may find surprising, found both a certain facility and a degree of real enjoyment in public speaking, taking me to a great variety of organisations, institutions and societies. Perhaps because of this I was approached by Rosemary Kelly, Secretary to the local Broadcasting Council, and asked if I would do the honours on this occasion.

I agreed the more readily in that I had at least met two of the principal players. I have earlier described my rather odd encounter years before with Duke Hussey, now Chairman of the BBC. His Vice Chairman, Joel Barnett, I had confronted on less social occasions. As Chief Secretary to the Treasury he had put in place a formula which continued to govern the distribution of Exchequer funding to Scotland and Northern Ireland. The term 'the Barnett formula' was often on the lips of my Department of Finance colleagues. While this issue of funding allocation had affected us all, I as a departmental Permanent Secretary had experience of a more direct and demanding interaction with him. He had become Chairman of the PAC, the Public Accounts Committee at Westminster. This is the place where sins will find you out, even if not committed by yourself personally. The first line of defence against a foolish or improper use of public money was the office of Comptroller and Auditor General (or C&AG). With full access not only to the accounts of a department but to all its files, the Comptroller could – and all too often did – discover evidence of something having gone badly wrong. As he drafted a report, one could argue about this or that; seek to point out a factual error or unfair inference. The Comptroller could take as much or as little account of such representations as he chose. On the basis of his published report, representing as it were 'the case for the prosecution', the PAC could decide whether it wished to hold hearings. There, in an intimidating Committee Room at the House of Commons, the Permanent Secretary of the responsible department, in his role of Accounting Officer for the public money voted to it, would find himself in the witness box if not in the dock. In the order of priorities for the pleasures of life, appearances at the PAC would be well down the list alongside root canal work without anaesthetic or the invitation on a visit to China to consume improbable organs of unidentifiable creatures.

In the circumstance I considered very carefully what I would say to the assembled company; Chairman, Vice Chairman, Governors, the Director General and his senior colleagues and my fellow local guests. Since my speech that evening, in the gracious surroundings of the Belfast Harbour Office, reflected my view of the BBC on the very eve of *unexpectedly* direct involvement with it, I propose to reproduce it here in full.

> It is always an agreeable thing to be entertained by the BBC. And like most of the sons and daughters of this age of radio and television, I *have* been entertained by the BBC just about every day for as long as I can remember. The Corporation does not, of course, always offer wine with that entertainment. That would be asking for too much and would point to a higher licence fee than even a more Keynesian approach to public expenditure would indicate.
>
> There emerges very clearly indeed in my memory, from over half a century ago, the recollection of my eight-year-old self listening to Neville Chamberlain declaring on the 'wireless' that we were at war with Germany. *ITMA* and Churchill broadcasts and the diffident voice of the late King were part of my growing up. On bitterly cold mornings just after the war, risking chilblains in our under-heated house, I would listen with bated breath to the rising and fading signals from Sydney or Melbourne where Australia were usually something like '1 for 159'; expressed wrong way round but all too clearly the voice of doom. Like so many other families we bought our first 'tele' for the Coronation. I listened to C. E. M. Joad on *The Brains Trust*

explaining how, until he had first heard his own recorded voice, he had always laboured under the illusion that he had a deep, manly tone. Piles of *The Listener* meanwhile accumulated on the floor of my bedroom-cum-study. Reading things one had missed on the BBC represented a kind of cultural smorgasbord, or perhaps sushi cut into small but brilliantly-coloured slices.

People expected a great deal of the BBC; indeed, almost as much as the BBC expected of itself. The choice of an Old Testament prophet as the initial presiding genius created echoes which reverberated for a very long time. The BBC was expected in some way not just to speak *to* the nation but also to a degree *for* the nation; to be a kind of improbable hybrid of the Delphic Oracle and the Archbishop of Canterbury. To be both conscience and communicator; to instruct and elevate as well as to amuse; to ensure that this nation at least still spoke not merely peace but truth unto other nations — all of that, as the management consultants would say, represents 'a demanding frame of reference'.

Happily, the BBC has always been able to draw upon a pool of exceptionally able and indeed remarkable people. I still vividly remember sitting at a university dinner in Coleraine next to Huw Wheldon, who was receiving an Honorary Doctorate, and being overwhelmed by his exuberant flow of wit and wisdom, accompanied as it was by playful but fairly painful punches which he used to give added emphasis to his arguments.

I think, too, of the wonderfully heterogeneous collection of people who, over the years, have held the post of National Governor for Northern Ireland; Dick Pim, Henry Dunleath, Bill O'Hara, Jim Kincade.

You and I first met, Chairman, at the home of Tim Willis, then Managing Director of the *Belfast Telegraph*. Your Vice Chairman I met in the rather less agreeable setting of the witness chair before the Select Committee of Public Accounts, of which he was a most formidable chairman. The chap who wrote recently that the three most stressful events in life were marriage, bereavement and moving house had clearly never served as the Accounting Officer of a government department. Unlike *Mastermind* one never moved away from special interest to general knowledge questions. And one had to wait thereafter for a verdict, because it was not the custom for members of the PAC to register any immediate marks either for technical merit or for artistic impression. I make the parallel because one was certainly skating on thin ice a good deal of the time.

And finally I might mention that I was one of those present at 'the

Battle of Culloden', although I took no part in the vigorous exchanges on that occasion, preferring for most of the time to hide under the tablecloth.

Chairman, I guess that both Northern Ireland and the BBC sometimes feel that their standards, role and performance are misunderstood. We are both obliged to carry out our work under a microscope of political, media or other scrutiny. You will appreciate that those of us who live and work here – most of us engaged, most of the time, in perfectly normal humdrum things like making goods or making families or making music – feel at times a bit like the patient in one of those old films featuring James Robertson Justice as the arrogant and insensitive surgical consultant. 'This,' he says, looking down at the patient on the bed with a faint air of contempt, 'is a particularly good peptic ulcer', and you can sense the patient muttering through clenched teeth 'No. This is a human being'. Just in the same way, we sometimes feel that we have to keep reminding the world that Northern Ireland is not just a 'security situation' but a complex living, striving society.

And you can help us, if I may say so, at three different levels, each of which is important. First, to see ourselves more clearly, for self-knowledge is the groundwork for analysis and effective action. We here can sometimes be over-sensitive to media investigation or academic research which draws attention to some less pleasant aspect of reality in a rather stark way.

Second, to help others to see us as we really are; and that means not just our problems and divisions, but also our splendours and opportunities and achievements.

And third, to help us to see others. The BBC offers a 'world service' not just in the sense of its output to the world, important though that is, but also in the sense of bringing the world to us. We are the first generation in human history to watch with our own eyes one of those historic tidal waves which change our world. Those who came before us could only read about 1798 and 1848 in the newspapers and some time after the events, with the impact dimmed by columns of tedious prose. Our ancestors could not be contemporary witnesses at the storming of the Bastille, but all of us could look on when the Wall was breached and the crowds gathered in the streets of Bucharest to tell Ceausescu his day was over. Let us not take any of this for granted: either the amazing technology or the still more amazing courage of professionals who chose to be there on our behalf.

One final thing I would wish to say. As a political imperative 'regionalism' in Britain tends to come and go. As one of our greatest national institutions the BBC has been consistently loyal to the idea of a strong regional presence and influence. It is far from being the case that every great institution in our national life admits a member from Northern Ireland to its governing body as a matter of right. It is far from being the case that every such institution accepts here its regional obligation, both to put excellence in and to take excellence out and offer it a wider audience. The Ulster accent is heard these days not just from Broadcasting House, Belfast but from many other places. 'Colespeak' has become the modern language of political commentary.

By way of explanation of these final words, I should explain that John Cole, who had risen to be Chief Political Correspondent of the BBC, whose unalloyed Ulster tones had become the subject of affectionate parody on *Spitting Image*, and whose heavy overcoat worn on wet evenings outside 10 Downing Street had achieved iconic status, had been a friend since those days in the Fifties when he had been a political correspondent for the *Belfast Telegraph* at Stormont and I had been Private Secretary to the Minister of Finance. He might well, I guess, have become editor of the *Guardian* if his line on Ulster, based on some real knowledge of the place, had not been against the ideological mind-set of the paper. It was odd that such an outstanding and scholarly writing journalist had to make his name in another medium. I could recall visiting him at the offices of the paper before we went off to have dinner at the 'Gay Hussar' in Soho. In the absence of the editor that day, John was in charge. I remember him saying: 'Do you mind waiting a few minutes? I've got to put the paper to bed'. I felt like an actor in some black-and-white Hollywood movie.

John's career at the BBC was not impeded by his undiluted Ulster accent, and indeed broadcasting journalists from Northern Ireland were to become peculiarly useful during the Falklands campaign. People born in Northern Ireland have the right to hold either or both British and Irish passports. Understandably journalists holding British passports were not conspicuously welcome in Buenos Aires as the Argentines struggled to maintain 'their' Malvinas. Suddenly Northern Ireland journalists of impeccably British sympathies and orientation found it convenient to seek and use Irish passports.

When I revisit today the Harbour Office speech of 1990 I am struck by the emergence of an image of the BBC's role which I was to use and refine during my term as a Governor. My 'last words' in the written mode were those used in BBC Northern Ireland's published 'Annual Review 98/99'. Writing a foreword to such a Review for the last time I observed:

> From time to time I have characterised the role of the BBC in Northern Ireland as being both a mirror and a window; a mirror in which this community can see itself clearly, and a window through which we look out upon Great Britain and the world, and through which they may see us in all our diversity and variety.

The speech as a whole could almost be read as the manifesto of an incoming Governor. No such thought had entered my head. I could not know that evening how events were to develop, or how soon.

2

AN UNEXPECTED OPPORTUNITY

Less than a week after the Governors' visitation and the Harbour Office dinner, the local Controller of the BBC, Revd Colin Morris, asked if he could call to see me at Stormont. Morris was an exotic in terms of BBC management; a minister of religion who had spent considerable time in Africa (where he had become a friend of Kenneth Kaunda) and who had initially risen through the hierarchy of religious broadcasting. An Englishman, a powerful preacher and eloquent broadcaster in his own right, he had earned real respect within the BBC locally and nationally and within the wider Northern Ireland community.

When we met it became clear that the purpose of his visit was to begin the process of identifying a new National Governor for Northern Ireland in succession to Dr James Kincade, who was due to retire later that year. I was a little surprised by this approach, since BBC Governors were chosen by the government (prior to appointment by the Queen in Council) rather than the Corporation. My limited experience of earlier appointments was that the Northern Ireland Office would offer some suggestions at the invitation of the responsible department, the Home Office. In turn it was natural that a key figure in framing NIO advice would be its Second Permanent Under Secretary, the Head of the Northern Ireland Civil Service, who could draw on years of experience of local events and personalities. Moreover in that role he was the supervisor of the work of the Central Appointments Unit (CAU) at Stormont Castle, which retained records of those who had been recommended, or had recommended themselves, as suitable for appointment to public office. This was no small task, since our small jurisdiction replicated on a modest scale much of the machinery of a great nation state, with commissions, boards and assorted quangos almost too numerous to mention. We were, indeed, at that time in the grip of a process actually adding to the number of public bodies, as government departments hived off 'agencies' and Health Boards contracted out their treatment work to an extensive network of hospital trusts.

So, as I say, it was not unusual or unexpected to be involved, although I would have anticipated an approach to originate from the Home Office rather than the BBC, let alone its local arm. Of course this whole culture of private sounding and discreet advice has long since (and quite rightly) been replaced by more transparent procedures. When my successor Fabian Monds became (as it happens) the last in the line of National Governors, it was at the conclusion of a process which involved public advertisement of the vacancy and objective interview.

What Morris wanted to do at this stage was to 'run past me' some names under consideration, although it was not clear whether or not this was at the direct request of the Home Office. At any rate he mentioned to me a number of names. Northern Ireland is in many ways a very small, intimate and closely-knit society, and it was no surprise to find that these individuals not only featured on the CAU list, but were without exception well-known to me. As best I could, I offered Morris my frank opinion on the abilities, experience and qualifications of each.

The discussion then took a wholly unexpected turn. Would I, Morris asked, wish to be considered for the position myself? My immediate response was that I would not be available to follow Kincade at the completion of his term. I would not be 60 (then the civil service retirement age) for another year, and I fully intended to remain at my post until the last day. I had not allowed the IRA's assassination attempt to displace me; nor would I consider leaving prematurely even if offered such a fascinating opportunity. Morris then asked a hypothetical question. If the incumbent's term were to be extended for a further year, would I then feel free to consider such an offer?

I decided that the right thing to do would be to tell Morris that I would certainly give serious consideration to such an offer, if made at a time when I would be free to accept it. In the meantime I would advise my 'opposite number', the PUS at the Northern Ireland Office, of this approach and ask to be excluded from any further consideration of the vacancy.

The truth of the matter is that I was not at all sure about what I would do after leaving the civil service where I had served since 1952. I would certainly take a lengthy holiday with Elizabeth to 'wind down' after so many years of heavy responsibility, but I did not intend to become one of those late risers ever more slowly walking the dog to pick up the morning paper. Some business opportunities might present themselves; but in spite of a term as Permanent Secretary at the Department of Economic Development I did not see myself as temperamentally well-adapted to the world of commerce and industry. Essentially I remained an 'ideas man' and a lover of the written and spoken word.

There was, however, one possible course which would rule me out from becoming National Governor. Professor Gerald Aylmer, Master of my old college, St Peter's at Oxford, was due to retire and after some soundings I decided to put my hat in the ring to succeed him. In due course I was shortlisted for interview by the Fellows. Looking back on it now I suspect that any prospect of success there was bound to be blighted by my obligation to tell them, in all fairness, that we had been under police protection since the attack on our home. In any case they had a very strong candidate from an academic background, the renowned classicist Professor John Barron, and they may well in any event have preferred a bona fide academic to a superannuated bureaucrat. Yet it was the case that many retired 'mandarins' had already become, or would become, Heads of Oxford colleges, including the admirable Robin Butler at University College and an old colleague from the Northern Ireland Office, Dennis Trevelyan, at Mansfield.

I am bound to say that, while disappointed by the outcome, I greatly enjoyed the arcane process itself, resembling as it did a scene from one of the novels of C. P. Snow. This included being conducted at one stage to a separate room to study the prescribed Oath of Office to satisfy myself that I could, if appointed, swear it in good conscience.

Most of all I recall a memorable ending to the day. After dining with the Fellows, I was making my way across the quadrangle to the guest room when I heard the unmistakable tones of Bach being played on the organ of the college chapel, formerly the Church of St Peter le Bailey (that is to say 'within the castle walls'). The chapel was in semi-darkness and the organist, the renowned medievalist Henry Mayr-Harting (later Regius Profesor of Ecclesiastical History) was at first unaware that I had crept in. When I made my presence known, he was kind enough to play some more.

Whether as a 'consolation prize' or for more meritorious reasons the college, having elected John Barron as their Master, appointed me an Honorary Fellow. Of course, if I had moved to Oxford I could never have become the BBC's National Governor for Northern Ireland. As it was, when I received an offer of the appointment from David Waddington, then the Home Secretary, I felt delighted and privileged to accept.

3

FIRST IMPRESSIONS OF THE BBC

Before taking up my appointment on 1st September 1991 I took the opportunity to meet key BBC staff in Belfast. Those most important to me would be the Regional Controller Robin Walsh, his Head of Programmes Pat Loughrey, the Head of Public Affairs Rosemary Kelly and her indefatigable assistant Nan Magee.

Robin, like myself a son of the Royal Belfast Academical Institution, had made his name in a range of important posts concerned with news and current affairs. Starting as a reporter with the *Belfast Telegraph* he had moved first to Ulster Television, the local commercial station, before joining the BBC in Belfast as News Editor in 1974. In the 1980s he had been a legendary Managing Editor for News and Current Affairs at BBC Television. He struck me as able but highly-strung; 'wired up' in the current fashionable expression. Given the image of newsmen as hard-bitten jacks of all trades, it was an odd fact that he had never learned to drive. Over time I had a growing sense that his promotion to Controller had not done him a favour. The highest ranks of many professions tend to involve turning one's back on one's true passions to concentrate on dreary issues of management; personnel problems, priorities and budgets. I myself had in many ways found the middle part of my career, with a hands-on responsibility for developing new policy and giving expression to it, far more enjoyable in many ways than serving as the professional head of the whole vast organisation. Vice Chancellors had told me how much they missed being directly involved in teaching and research; an Air Vice Marshal had bitterly confessed to me: 'I joined the RAF to fly planes, not to fly desks'. In the BBC itself

David Attenborough might well have become Director General, but opted to pursue a career at the programme-making coalface.

Robin Walsh I knew a little already. Pat Loughrey was quite new to me. He had made his way into broadcasting from the teaching profession, like that earlier and very distinguished Controller James Hawthorne. Beginning as a producer of educational programmes in 1984 after ten years as a schoolteacher, he had moved steadily through the Headship of Educational Broadcasting to the very important position of Head of Programmes across the whole range of the output.

It needs to be emphasised here that the depth of local programme-making involvement differed greatly as between radio and television. Radio Ulster offered a full, day-long service to local listeners, covering news and current affairs, speech and drama, music and entertainment. By many measures, it had the best audience share of any BBC regional or local station. On the other hand the television viewer in Northern Ireland would see for the most part on BBC1 and BBC2 diverse network programmes screened across the whole of the UK. Of course quite a number of local viewers, feeling a greater affinity with 'Irish' than with 'British' culture, would seek a means to view the programmes of RTE, the Irish state broadcaster (which itself drew upon popular British soaps in filling its schedules). Because television is a very expensive medium, and also because Northern Ireland viewers wished to view popular national programmes, Belfast's production effort for local consumption (whether produced 'in house' or commissioned from independents) would have a strong emphasis on news and current affairs. Since coverage of developments in Northern Ireland remained for years high on the national news agenda, many broadcasters began what developed into high profile careers at the front line in Belfast or Derry. In addition to the core coverage of news and current affairs, there would be coverage of major cultural events, high profile local sport and offerings of drama and entertainment. Then there would be the annual local input to 'Children in Need'. In the area of sport, rights were becoming increasingly expensive and the search for them more and more competitive. While BBC Northern Ireland produced more (and more diverse) television locally than its commercial competitor UTV, the ITV offering as a whole drew larger audiences than the

BBC offering, reflecting to some extent the socio-economic make-up of the local community. There was, of course, no reason why Belfast should produce only programmes for local transmission, and costly and elaborate programmes could only be justified by mass audiences. Local producers and executives would attempt to 'sell' to London local production ideas requiring central funding, but when I arrived in 1991 the Northern Ireland contribution to network television was minimal.

Rosemary Kelly, in her role as secretary to the Broadcasting Council, would represent a vital link between management and the Council which I would now chair. Both she and I would enjoy the wonderful support of Nan Magee, a mature married woman with the energy and zest of a teenager, whose idea of heaven was a hundred-mile bicycle ride and who seldom travelled the corridors of Broadcasting House other than at 'full speed ahead'.

On one of these early visits to Ormeau Avenue I was lucky enough to meet two of the principal and most interesting players from the heart of BBC management. Ron Neil, a burly, cheerful and engaging Glaswegian, had by then worked for the BBC for almost a quarter of a century. Newsreader, reporter, editor, Director of News and Current Affairs; he had done it all. On his CV were *Newsnight*, *That's Life*, *The Six O'Clock News*, and many other flagship programmes. Now, as Managing Director of Regional Broadcasting, Northern Ireland was part of his patch, and he would be a key figure in efforts to gain a better network foothold.

With him on this visit was Howell James, since 1987 the BBC's Director of Corporate Affairs. Charming, puckish, loquacious; James was no lightweight in the world of public relations and 'spin'. It would take a thoroughgoing professional to serve, as he did from 1994 to 1997, as Political Secretary to the Prime Minister (John Major) and be sufficiently respected across the political spectrum to be appointed in 2004, under the Blair government, Permanent Secretary for Government Communications. I shall have more to say later about relations between the BBC and the big world outside, not least the government of the day. Suffice it to say here that the 'corporate affairs' of the Corporation could be complex and controversial, and needed at all times to be handled with a light yet professional touch.

Another important contact in this run-in period was with the Secretary of the Corporation, John McCormick. He, too, had begun his working life as a schoolteacher, before joining the BBC in 1970. If Rosemary Kelly was the hyphen in Northern Ireland joining the Broadcasting Council and BBC management, so McCormick at the heart of the system represented a vital link between Governors and management, Chairman and Director General. Cheerful, efficient and straight as a die, McCormick had a key role to play and one requiring great diplomacy. I had some faint concept of the pitfalls of such a position, having occupied years before the office of Private Secretary in a government department where Minister and Permanent Secretary were barely on speaking terms. I did not imagine anything could be as bad at the BBC; experience would prove me wrong, as experience so often does.

Another diversion during this fallow period between leaving the public service and joining the BBC Board was to respond to various requests for interviews with me about my long and varied experience in government. I was not in a mood to 'tell tales' or hint at state secrets, but I felt I could be a little more open about crucial events, and greatly enjoyed extensive encounters with such legendary local broadcasters as Sam McAughtrie or Billy Flackes, the famed political correspondent widely and affectionately known as 'Billy Flack Jacket'. I could never recall without laughing a critical day in Northern Ireland's politics when the news broke that Brian Faulkner had resigned from Terence O'Neill's cabinet. Called to make instant comment on air, Billy was unfortunate enough to find the lifts malfunctioning. Sprinting up several flights of stairs, he arrived at the microphone so out of breath that the announcement 'And now over to W. D. Flackes' was followed by what seemed an eternity occupied only by the sort of heavy breathing encountered on the soundtrack of a blue movie.

I would attend my first meeting of the Board of Governors on 12th September. However this was preceded by my first visit to London as a Governor in the previous week. A full and fascinating day began with a meeting with David Hatch, Managing Director of Network Radio, followed by breakfast with David and the Radio Controllers (of BBC Radio 1, 2, 3 and 4). Hatch had been one of that generation at

Cambridge which produced a galaxy of comic performers, and indeed he himself might easily have become a Michael Palin. Inspirational, eloquent, witty, entertaining, the heart and soul of BBC Radio, I took to David Hatch at once and never had any reason to alter my view. In mid-morning I attended the Radio Review Board, where the makers of programmes entertained the comments, critical or complimentary, of their peers. Thereafter I had a discussion at lunch with Jenny Abramsky, the formidably intelligent Head of News and Current Affairs for BBC Radio.

The following week it would be the turn of the television side of the BBC empire, with a visit to the Television Centre at Wood Lane to meet Will Wyatt, Managing Director of Network Television, attend a Television Review Board and see something of the organisation and infrastructure required to transmit news and weather bulletins, *Wogan* or *Top of the Pops* and a huge spectrum of other programmes and genres. It was not my first visit to this great 'fun factory'. Accompanying O'Neill I had dined there years before with television mandarins, and later on a visit to London with Elizabeth we had been in the audience at the *Parkinson Show*. As we sat in the audience waiting for the great man to appear, I confessed to Elizabeth my total frustration at not yet having heard the result of a crucial rugby international that afternoon, with Ireland playing for the legendary Triple Crown. Obligingly the man immediately in front, who had heard this exchange, volunteered the good news that Ireland had defeated Scotland and won the mythical Crown; thereafter revealing that he was in fact, Parkinson's father, up in town to see his son's show.

I had also noticed in one of the offices at the Television Centre a framed costume design prepared by my cousin John Bloomfield, a successful costume designer for cinema, television and the stage. The costume depicted was one of those designed for the hugely successful *Six Wives of Henry VIII* starring Keith Michell as 'the merry Monarch' (merry, that is, unless you were foolish enough to marry him). For this he had received a BAFTA award. John had a flair for using contemporary materials (often bits of scrap or cloth sprayed with silver or gold paint) to replicate the costumes of the relevant period, carefully researched from original sources. If you wanted someone to construct the regalia of a Lord Chancellor from a length of lavatory chain, appropriately gilded, John was your man. So popular were both the drama and the costumes that the latter were put on public display, with large crowds turning up to see them. I understand that the relevant curator at the V&A plaintively complained: 'We have the finest collection of real Tudor costumes in the world, and very few people ever come to see them.' An illustration of the awesome power of television!

Next day, then, 12th September 1991, I attended the first of my many meetings as a BBC Governor and at last encountered my new colleagues, Governors and senior management, in action.

As I have already explained, I had met the Chairman, Duke Hussey, many years before. He had welcomed me to the Board with a characteristic comment: 'I'm afraid we can't pay you very much in this job, old boy, but as long as I'm here you'll always enjoy a decent glass of wine.' Dukie was physically impressive, enormously tall and craggy, and seemingly impervious to the pain and incessant discomfort of a fearful wartime injury incurred at a very early age and most bravely borne. It pleased the smart-alecs within and without the Corporation to portray him as a silly old buffer, but I doubt if many of these snide critics would have shrugged off his disabilities with such sangfroid. In some respects he reminded me of one of my former political masters, Willie Whitelaw, the first Secretary of State for Northern Ireland. The 'silly old buffer' image was no more than a smokescreen. Dukie had survived in the shark pool with Rupert Murdoch, even though his time at Times Newspapers had been a turbulent and difficult one.

I supposed, as I set out on my course at the BBC, that I would mainly encounter him at formal meetings of the Board and that otherwise he would contact me only in cases of extreme urgency and complexity. Only over time did I learn (and admire) his methods. A chairman of a great company or public body can choose from various options to ensure that he gets his way more often than not. He can be a despot, riding roughshod over opposition, and I would later experience, if not enjoy, leadership of this flavour. On the other hand he can be a diplomat, always courteous, persuasive, bringing colleagues along more or less willingly rather than driving them like a flock of sheep. Hussey was to prove a master of these latter mysteries. With quite surprising frequency, late in the evening or during the weekend, Dukie would phone one at home. Just a word, he would suggest, with a very few of his particularly close and trusted colleagues. Only over time did one suspect that, almost certainly, all the members of the Board would have received a very similar call.

Of course any Chairman worth his salt would want and expect to get his own way more often than not. Yet, in an interesting way, I came to see the governance of the BBC as presenting some parallels with modes of governing the country. I had worked in a Cabinet Secretariat, albeit in a small if troublesome jurisdiction; I had devoured the standard works on cabinet government while reading Modern History at Oxford; and saw the classic description of the Prime Minister as *primus inter pares* as defining a role embracing collegiality as well as leadership. Governors were not appointed to the BBC Board to be mere cohorts of the Chairman; Hussey preferred the arts of persuasion to the *fuhrerprinzip*.

Given his social background and relationships, it was a reasonable assumption that Hussey's views were fundamentally conservative in character. In an effort, not always successful, to escape criticism of covert political influence, it had become established practice to appoint a Vice Chairman from 'the opposite camp'. Anyone reading Joel Barnett's CV would have seen him as the ideal political foil. A product of the striving and thriving Manchester Jewish community, Joel's long political career as a Labour MP had carried him to the chairmanship of the PAC and membership of the cabinet as Chief Secretary of the Treasury and principal guardian of the national purse-strings. However, while always socialist he could hardly have been described as radical. He and Hussey had forged a very close relationship, uniting, for example, to dismiss Alasdair Milne from the Director Generalship with some decisive brutality. Significantly, Barnett had an office at Broadcasting House, and clearly was a great deal more than merely a person who would chair a Board meeting in the absence of Hussey.

In my Belfast speech of 1990 I had referred to the fact that the BBC Charter guaranteed Northern Ireland of a place on the Board. The Corporation (for in law the Governors were the BBC) consisted of twelve members in all. Seven of these were Governors at large, with no specific territorial responsibility or commitment. Nevertheless, government commonly touched certain bases in making these appointments. With a large and unionised workforce, it would be useful to benefit from the perspective of an experienced trade union leader of the sensible tendency. Since part of the Corporation's output, funded for this purpose by the Foreign and Commonwealth Office, was directed to areas of the world far from the United Kingdom, an experienced retired diplomat could have a valuable contribution to make. In an increasingly multicultural Britain, some representation of ethnic minorities would demonstrate a desirable recognition of diversity. As a broadcaster of orchestral music, opera, ballet, plays and films the Board would greatly benefit from the presence of some acknowledged expertise from the cultural world. It was, of course, possible that one or more of the National Governors would help to tick these boxes.

The Chairman and Vice Chairman both had permanent bases at Broadcasting House, and were expected to devote a very substantial part of their time to the work of the Corporation. Each of the three National Governors, remunerated at the same level as the Vice Chairman, enjoyed accommodation and staff support within their 'national' headquarters. (There were problems of nomenclature here. Scotland would be happy to be termed a 'nation', Wales was a 'principality', Northern Ireland 'Ulster' or 'the province' to the unionist majority, and 'the six counties' or 'the north of Ireland' to the nationalist minority. Hence the designation of a corporate empire of 'nations and regions', allowing some ambiguity about which was which.)

How, then, did the Board I joined in 1991 meet these implicit criteria? John Parry, the National Governor for Wales, completed his term of office before I had a chance to know him well, although I appreciated and still remember a warm welcome and some good advice as I arrived. My first Scottish equivalent was Sir Graham Hills, an academic chemist and former Vice Chancellor at the University of Strathclyde. Graham was a wonderfully entertaining if sometimes unpredictable character. Short, animated and cheery, he had the attractive characteristics of one of those perky robins who perch on the handle of your spade during a pause in gardening. He was a regular and consummate writer of letters to *The Times*, often on issues of higher education, and these were invariably tart, witty and idiosyncratic.

In those days Governors travelling to London meetings from a distance, and needing to stay overnight prior to an early start, would often be booked by the BBC into the Langham Hotel, literally across the road from Broadcasting House. The hotel seemed to be used as a training ground for young and personable men and women being groomed by the Hilton organisation for managerial posts elsewhere. More often than not, the smart young man or woman at the reception desk would be Swiss or Italian or even Japanese. In the modern world of the 'hospitality industry' computerised records alert the staff to the fact that an arriving guest has stayed in the hotel before. Trained to be the warm and welcoming voice of the Hilton Group, the smart young receptionist would smile graciously. 'Nice to see you again, Sir Bloomfield. And nice to see you again, Sir Hills.' Graham would assume his Vice-Chancellorial expression. 'Pause a moment, if you will, and let me explain to you the elements of English social usage.' There would follow a brilliant, lucid and exhaustive mini-lecture on appropriate modes of address. The recipient would bow his or her head with an expression of gratitude and appreciation, before replying 'Thank you very much, Sir Hills.' At least he did not have to cope with my own occasional experience of finding my place-card at a formal dinner describing me as 'Sir Kenneth Bloomfield KGB'. I would then have to point out that I had been at Oxford rather than Cambridge.

The 'ordinary Governors' at the time were Dr John Roberts, a distinguished academic historian; Baroness James (the renowned crime writer, P. D. James); Bill Jordan from Birmingham, a moderate and sensible trade union leader and president of the AEU; Keith Oates, Deputy Chairman of Marks and Spencer; Dr Jane Glover, a well-known music scholar and conductor of orchestral and choral music; Shahwar Sadeque, a Muslim of Bangladeshi origins and an expert on 'artificial intelligence'; and Lord Nicholas Gordon-Lennox, a former ambassador at Madrid and a member of the ducal family of Richmond and Gordon. Not perhaps, very representative of the mass audience out there; largely middle-aged and middle-class. On the other hand, not a conglomeration of idiots, poodles, clones or tools of the Conservative government then in power. As I came to know them better, I learned that it is possible to be a faithful Muslim without being intolerant; that it is possible to be an aristocrat and distinguished diplomat without being snobbish or self-important; that a woman of high principle, like P. D. James, can act as a kind of moral spirit level.

At my first meeting of the Board I learned that these affairs were far from being an intimate chat amongst a group of a dozen people. Ranged around the large hollow table in the Council Chamber would be not only the twelve Governors but the Director General (DG) and other members of the Board of Management, the Secretary John McCormick and his deputy and sundry other flankers and outriders. The Governors and senior managers would alternate around the table. If one sat opposite the Chairman, one would gaze across a large empty space, and there were to be occasions when I felt this might usefully have been occupied by a big tank of piranha fish. As it was, some of the piranhas were seated at the table.

In some organisations the Chief Executive is a member of the board; indeed, he or she may be Chairman as well as Chief Executive. This had not been the practice at the BBC, but of course the DG was bound to be a powerful presence and major influence at meetings of the Board.

I had just emerged from the world of the civil service, involving me in regular and close interaction with members of the cabinet and other ministers. As Head of the Civil Service in Northern Ireland I had waged an unremitting but not wholly successful campaign to urge upon colleagues the need for concision and brevity. Ministers, I reminded them, were exceptionally busy people. They could be overwhelmed, indeed drowned, by paper; on occasions, one felt, this could be a deliberate and cynical tactic to smuggle some proposal or policy past an antipathetic minister. Our political masters, I persistently argued, should be told what they truly needed to know to reach a well-informed decision; but it should not be taken as an opportunity for the briefing official to display the whole range of his vast (yet sometimes irrelevant) accumulated knowledge. 'Let me have on one sheet of paper', the wartime Churchill would dictate. In the last resort detail of marginal relevance could be relegated to an annexe.

Against the background of this experience in government, I found the prolixity of the BBC astonishing. In one of the world's leading media of communication, Governors would be inundated before each meeting by masses of paper. Not only would we receive voluminous material from the management, but regular doses of press coverage of our affairs, inches thick. It became clear that every move the BBC made was a matter of close press attention, not least from papers whose media stable-mates were radio and/or television stations. At the Board meeting itself, management seemed strangely reluctant to accept that its circulated papers had been read and understood. So we would often have to endure a PowerPoint presentation of much the same material, with hard copy to follow in case our tiny minds had failed to grasp the arguments when presented the first two times.

I found this all the more irritating because I continued to live in a protected environment. When horses escape, doors are rapidly bolted at empty stables. So the home we occupied from 1990 had all the para-phernalia of automatic gates, security lighting, entry-activated beams and other ingenious devices. As no postman could be permitted to approach our front door, a mail box was provided outside our entry gates. Unhappily it was not designed for the reception of BBC agenda papers resembling a volume of the *Encyclopaedia Britannica*, and so these bundles, thrust into the narrow aperture by main force, would often arrive in a rather crumpled state.

I might add that, because of my security status, I would be driven to Belfast International Airport at Aldergrove by my RUC escorts, held in a VIP suite and brought out to the plane at the last moment. I would travel under an assumed name, which was changed for each visit. On return to Belfast via Heathrow the drill was that I would be driven to a check-point, where I would give my 'name of the day', be passed through to the Hounslow hospitality suite and from there driven out to the Belfast plane. Unhappily events did not always proceed according to plan. 'Smith' or 'Robinson' or 'Green', I would pronounce through the car window. The security man would turn over page after page on his flip-sheet. 'Don't see you here, mate', he would say with that peculiar smugness exhibited by a jack-in-office erecting an unnecessary and unwelcome hurdle. I would then sit fuming in the car before multiple telephone calls would establish that notification of my imminent arrival had been delayed 'in the interests of security'.

So much for the Governors. The Board of Management, only one less in number that the Board of Governors, was of course headed by the Director General, Michael Checkland and his Deputy, John Birt. We then had four Managing Directors; John Tusa for the World Service, David Hatch for Network Radio, Ron Neil for Regional Broadcasting and Will Wyatt for Network Television. Alongside them sat four Directors; Bill Dennay for Engineering, Howell James for Corporate Affairs, Ian Phillips for Finance and Margaret Salmon for Personnel. James Arnold-Baker completed the senior management team as Chief Executive of BBC Enterprises.

I soon learned that I had strayed into a minefield, which had been sown by a most unfortunate decision of the Board of Governors prior to my appointment. Mike Checkland's appointment to the Director Generalship in 1987 had, perhaps, been something of a surprise. With a background in accountancy, Checkland had flourished as an invaluable ally of the redoubtable Bill Cotton in the battle for resources to fund Cotton's ambitions for BBC1, leading to his appointment to become Director of Resources for the whole of BBC Television in 1982, followed by promotion to Deputy Director General in 1985. When, in 1987, Alasdair Milne 'resigned' the post of DG after Hussey and Barnett had offered him the unappealing option of being fired (the Governors generally having lost confidence in him), Checkland was left to hold the fort as Acting Director General. The vacancy was duly advertised, and emerging candidates included David Dimbleby, Michael Grade, Jeremy Isaacs and Brian Wenham. With a distinct division of opinion within the Board about Dimbleby and Isaacs, Checkland slipped through the middle, but with considerable reservations on the part of Hussey. He received a five-year contract which would expire in 1992. As this date grew nearer, Checkland understandably sought from the Board clarification of his post-1992 position, making it clear that he was willing to serve a further term. By mid-1991, however, John Birt had established himself as an extremely powerful and assertive Deputy Director General. On the one hand, then, Checkland was keen to serve for a further full term, and had performed solidly if not spectacularly. On the other, Birt was aching to succeed him, unwilling to contemplate waiting for another six years, and likely if disappointed to seek employment elsewhere. Once more the Board found itself split down the middle. The outcome was a grotesque fudge. Checkland would be offered an extension until 1993, at which point Birt would succeed him.

This most unhappy compromise was open to serious objection on two fronts. It would require almost superhuman patience and tolerance for the unfortunate Checkland to soldier on into 1993 with his designated successor looking over his shoulder, and with other managers inevitably looking more and more to the rising than the setting sun. This was bad enough. But if Checkland was to be replaced, one would have expected a transparent appointment process to parallel that used at the time of his own appointment: public advertisement inviting applications from all and sundry inside or outside the Corporation. Someone of the experience and intellectual weight of John Tusa may or may not have won the appointment, although his triumphant later success at the Barbican Centre demonstrated real powers of management coupled with creative imagination. It was quite wrong that one of the most influential positions in our national life should have been filled as an 'inside job', without any competition or objective consideration of alternatives. Checkland had taken this kick in the teeth like a gentleman, but it was hardly surprising that over time his ambiguous position became less and less tolerable.

Before outlining the other principal challenges facing the Corporation when I joined it in 1991, it is necessary to understand the constitutional framework and political realities within which the BBC was operating. On the face of it the Corporation was a body enjoying a remarkable degree of independence. Endowed on the one hand with a compulsory licence fee paid by all those in possession of radio or television sets, the Corporation represented by its Governors, appointed by the Queen in Council and effectively irremovable in the absence of unthinkable contingencies, was not controlled by the government and was much less influenced by it than public service broadcasters in other countries. Certainly crude and overt interference was unlikely. This did not, though, mean a total absence of pressure and implicit threat behind the scenes. In more recent times the constant nagging of Alastair Campbell became notorious, but in earlier days Conservatives like Norman Tebbit could be relied upon to keep a constant beady eye on the activities of the Corporation. Honest and fearless journalism will inevitably focus upon those who are doing important things. Governments do, and Oppositions talk. Thus any criticism of health or education or military strategy will inevitably focus upon those in charge of such things in real time. The longer a government of any political persuasion is in power, the more paranoid it will become about attacks on its competence and bona fides. The known or suspected Labour sympathies of senior BBC players, far from tempering a Labour government's reaction to criticism, merely sour it with a sense of betrayal.

Moreover, if government could not rein in the BBC day by day, it could shape or constrain its future at critical times. At the end of his first term a Governor could either be re-appointed or replaced. At regular intervals the Charter and Licence framing the governance of the Corporation fell to be reviewed, updated and revised (potentially in a more restrictive sense). Government, sometimes of its own volition and sometimes after external review, would set the forward trajectory of the licence fee at, above or below the expected rate of inflation.

Indeed the BBC, for obvious reasons, had many enemies and critics. Commercial broadcasters, including some with wider media interests and influential political contacts, constantly sought to cry 'unfair competition' and confine the BBC to a restricted corral of serious and worthy programme-making unappealing to mass audiences. And of course, as TV channels proliferated, particularly on the incoming tide of the 'digital revolution', one could expect many licence-payers to watch BBC television less and less and object more and more to paying the licence fee. Yet no one had been able to identify a plausible alternative as capable as the licence fee of sheltering the BBC from commercial, political and other pressures. Later I would play, with Lord Nicholas Gordon-Lennox, a leading role in seeking to clarify the key purposes of the Board of Governors. In high-falutin' language we were 'trustees for the public interest'. More demotically, our job was to see that the Corporation was not pushed around. We shall see later how pressures from politicians could have an effect opposite to that intended.

Of course a particularly critical relationship was that between the BBC and the political head of the government department responsible for broadcasting. This had long been the Home Office, but would later be the Department of National Heritage, headed successively by David Mellor, Peter Brooke my old boss at the Northern Ireland Office, Stephen Dorrell and Virginia Bottomley. Under 'New Labour' the torch would pass to Chris Smith. On the occasion of the annual Board conference, the contemporary Secretary of State would join the Governors at dinner for some frank exchanges. It has to be said that, of all the ministers who played this role, David Mellor made the most favourable impression on me. It helped that he himself had a real cultural hinterland, as displayed later by his masterful presentation of music on Classic FM, but he also gave us some sage and honest advice which contributed to our escape from the jaws of death. Margaret Thatcher in particular, with the enthusiastic support and urging of the ineffable Denis, had loathed and detested the BBC as an anti-competitive, bureaucratic, corporatist and insufferably left-wing conspiracy. But for the restraining influence of such as William Whitelaw and Douglas Hurd she would happily have castrated or abolished the Corporation long before.

As I arrived on the scene in 1991, a massive internal exercise to prepare for 'Charter renewal' was under way. In an attempt to escape from the established wisdom of distinctive parts of the organisation, concerned with education or religion or sport or entertainment, fifteen separate 'task forces' had been established, each of them chaired by a person outside the normal line of responsibility for that aspect of the output. The idea was to 'think outside the box'; to re-examine critically and from first principles every aspect of BBC activity. In the background lurked the issue of whether the Corporation should continue to operate across such a comprehensive range of genres and tastes, or retreat to some mythical Himalayan height of self-evident excellence. As the reports emerged, my own sympathy was with the many trees which must have been felled in virgin forests to produce such a mountain of speculation and hypothesis. What seemed to be emerging, though, was a consensus that the BBC should operate within much the same territory but from the high ground. We would not abandon game shows, but they would be *excellent* game shows. We would not cease to broadcast rock and pop, but we would somehow elevate and enhance them. Inevitably the modern BBC found itself on the horns of a dilemma. If it abandoned to the commercial sector those broadcasting activities of particular interest to the younger generation of viewers and listeners, they might over time become more and more alienated from the Corporation and its heavier-weight programmes. The Reithian offering, of a single radio service which people accessed to indulge known tastes but stayed tuned to sample, and perhaps become attached to, previously unknown diversions, was no longer valid. Radio 1 and Radio 3 would retain the loyalty, by and large, of separate and distinct audiences. There was a growing tendency to outpost events of high culture to BBC2, enhancing the positioning of BBC1 as a channel concentrating on the attraction of mass audiences.

Where, in all of this, was one to place a 'soap' like *Eastenders*? Audience figures for this and its commercial television counterparts consistently showed high levels of popularity and massive audiences in all parts of the country. The story lines were often implausible. Drug addiction, rape, murder, abortion – all of these things, as newspapers testified, occurred in real life as well as on the small screen. Yet in a real East End or Wetherfield there would be days of humdrum tedium, with only occasional episodes of excitement, tragedy or disaster. So were the broadcasters in general, and the BBC in particular, 'dumbing down' to pander to the assumed tastes of their audiences? In this area I was happy to accept that, however tawdry and improbable many of the storylines, the pace of the narrative and the high quality of performance could carry the day. I had grown up reading the entire oeuvre of Dickens, purchased by my parents in the 1930s in a cheap fake-morocco-bound edition sponsored by a national newspaper. From spontaneous combustion to cobweb-strewn wedding cakes many of his novelistic situations were implausible. Some of his most famous works had been in a real sense the forerunners of the 'soaps'; published in instalments, leaving the reader in suspense at the end of a chapter and bringing the hero or heroine to a happy ending after improbable trials.

I recall that in my first week at Oxford as a raw and innocent 18-year-old from Belfast, I had received an invitation from a Fellow of All Souls (Charles Monteith, an old boy of my grammar school and later chairman of Faber and Faber) to join him at lunch in this academic pantheon. Seated with luminaries like Professor G. D. H. Cole and Sir Sarvepalli Radhakrishnan (later President of India) I was totally out of my depth, in terms of confidence if not of intelligence, and prudently decided to say as little as possible. Towards the end of the meal, gaining a modest degree of false confidence, I dared to mention with favour one of those obscure continental movies which were the staple diet of a particular Oxford cinema. 'How interesting,' ventured one ancient polymath, 'I never go to the cinema.'

I began to suspect that some of my Board colleagues never watched *Eastenders*, and ignored the reality that it attracted far more viewers than any other BBC programme. I decided the least one could do was to show some interest and appreciation, and so Elizabeth and I spent the best part of a day on the set, met all the principal actors and admired the way in which a cramped location was transformed on screen into a whole bustling neighbourhood.

Over time we also had the privilege of being present on occasions of a cultural and celebratory kind: the Last Night of the Proms, Young Musician of the Year, Cardiff Singer of the World, and others. I remember that we were joined at the Cardiff event by Norma Major, wife of the then Prime Minister, and very knowledgeable about opera. Where a First Lady of the United States would no doubt have been delivered to a comparable event in a bulletproof limousine, surrounded by men wearing dark glasses and simulated hearing-aids, Mrs Major had driven herself down from London unaccompanied and in her own modest private car.

I was fortunate enough, in the middle of my first month on the Board, to attend a signal event in the life of BBC Northern Ireland, the inauguration in Belfast by Michael Checkland of the Blackstaff Studio, the last purpose-built BBC television studio to open before concentration and retrenchment became the order of the day. A Gala Show in the new studio that evening was to be the first of many visits to Blackstaff, either to be present at some special event like Children in Need or as a programme participant.

September also saw my first meeting as Chairman of the Broadcasting Council which for the next eight years would play an important part in my life. The members at that time included an eloquent and articulate legal academic called Mary McAleese. She would soon leave us to join the Board of Channel 4, but it is not given to everyone to chair a future Head of State, with Mary becoming a most popular and admired President of Ireland in 1997.

September 1991 was, indeed, to prove a full and fascinating introductory month. Not only had I encountered Board and management colleagues for the first time, helped to 'dine out' my predecessor, attended my first Board meeting and been present at the inauguration of a new studio, but found myself in the improbable surroundings of Milton Keynes. Here were situated the headquarters of the Open University, probably the most enduring legacy of the Wilson government, and conceived as a bold experiment in 'distance learning', harnessing BBC experience to make inexpensive but informative programmes as televised lectures or tutorials. The visit began with a dinner at the residence of the Vice Chancellor, Sir John Daniel, and on the following day we visited the OU Production Centre and had lunch with Open University staff as well as fitting in a meeting of the Board.

Later, as the first Chairman of the Northern Ireland Higher Education Council, I would take every opportunity to underline the importance and uniqueness, in our community as elsewhere, of the Open University. It had become a most powerful instrument for people in mid-career to top up their professional qualifications, or to satisfy a yearning for higher learning which circumstances had withheld from them at an earlier stage in life. Our Council, which was launched in 1993, was specifically concerned with institutions locally funded (which the OU was not), but I made a point of keeping in close touch with Rosemary Hamilton, the OU director for Ireland, and was often a guest at local graduation ceremonies. On one such occasion the graduation had taken place in the Whitla Hall of Queen's University, after which special guests were to be entertained to lunch in that university's Senior Common Room, across the road from the main campus. On arrival at the building hosting the lunch, the Honorary Graduate of the day, an Ulsterman distinguished for his humanitarian work, his elderly mother, Lady Daniel the wife of the Vice Chancellor, Elizabeth and I summoned the lift to take us to the upper floor where lunch was to be served. We then encountered an embarrassing problem. In a university distinguished for mechanical engineering the lift became irretrievably stuck between floors. Our failure to turn up seemed to arouse no curiosity. Eventually, after a great deal of banging and shouting, a university handyman responded to our ever more plaintive appeals. All else having failed, we were eventually rather ignominiously rescued by a unit of the Fire Brigade. When we arrived, dishevelled and belatedly, for the graduation lunch it could truly be said that we had made our way by small degrees. Today I too am an Honorary Doctor of the Open University, and the peacock inside me rather enjoys the occasional outing in fancy dress.

I might add that the longer one lives the more one finds the world is a very small place. Readers of Anthony Powell's great series of novels, *A Dance to the Music of Time* sometimes criticise what they see as the improbability of various characters cropping up again and again in unexpected places and situations. Yet one of my duties when chairman of the Northern Ireland Higher Education Council was to meet periodically with the chairs and chief executives of the several Funding Councils for England, Scotland and Wales. And who, from 1997 to 2001, was the Chairman of HEFCE, the Higher Education Funding Council for England? Michael Checkland, former Director General of the BBC.

4

THE CORONATION OF JOHN BIRT

I have explained that, initially at least, Checkland had reacted in a dignified way to his hole-in-corner displacement by John Birt and the prospect of a difficult and uncomfortable interregnum. For his part, Birt made every effort to give Checkland his (inevitably diminished) place. He was, of course, involved in such issues as reacting to the views and recommendations of the several task forces, but much of his time was being spent on reflection, and in close colloquy with consultants from McKinsey, the internationally active advisers on business practices.

John Birt had a strange, shy, veiled and uncommunicative personality. He was a son of Liverpool and a product of a Christian Brothers education there. Things may or may not have been different in England, but in Ireland the Christian Brothers had the reputation of being strict and rigid disciplinarians, intolerant of idiosyncrasy or dissent. On going up to Oxford (St Catherine's College) he opted, like many others before and after him, to read for a degree (in his case in Engineering), which failed to engage his interest or exploit his talents. At the early age of 21 he had married a charming American, Jane Lake, an artist of some ability. By his mid-twenties he had become well established in independent television, where he was involved in the production of a number of prestigious programmes, including *World in Action*, *The Frost Programme*, *Weekend World* and *The Nixon Interview*. As a senior executive at London Weekend Television (LWT) he had made useful contacts with Christopher Bland, Peter Mandelson and others. Ironically, his recruitment by the BBC owed not a little to Michael Grade, one of the unsuccessful aspirants for the post of DG after Milne's 'resignation'. Checkland, essentially from a background of finance and administration rather than radio or TV production per se, recognised the need for a capable deputy who would bring to the top table complementary skills, particularly in the area of news and current affairs. Partly at least on the basis of Grade's recommendation Checkland decided to attract Birt, if he could, to join the BBC. Here was an irony of truly Shakespearian dimensions, since Birt, once in place, would put Grade's nose out of joint and lead to the truncation of Checkland's career. As Deputy Director General Birt effectively elbowed Grade, who regarded himself as a senior and more experienced figure in the broadcasting business, out of the way, leading to his departure for Channel 4.

Since the nature of Birt's commitment to the BBC would in time become a matter of intense controversy, it should be emphasised that, in my view, power and influence mattered much more to him than money. BBC salaries, which could seem astronomical when publicised in populist newspapers, were at that time if anything below the industry norm for the most senior executives. Not only did Birt accept a reduction in salary on joining the BBC, but he missed out on the bonanza from which Bland and others profited on the takeover of LWT.

In his introverted and rather withdrawn way Birt had a rare ability for cultivating the friendship of talented people on the rise. Some of these stood the test of time, while others buckled under the pressure of events and the force of this quiet man's driving ambition and focused single-mindedness. A scan of the photographs published in Birt's autobiography *The Harder Path* (a rather revealing title) reveals pictures of John walking on the Brecon Beacons with Terry Burns, trekking in New Zealand with Robin Butler, playing football with Greg Dyke or go-karting with Christopher Bland and Peter Mandelson. An ultimate life peerage and appointment to an ill-defined role as 'Strategy Adviser' to Tony Blair would be testimony to a certain genius for networking.

From his appointment as Director General-Designate in July 1991 there opened up the prospect of an awkward interregnum stretching forward almost two years until Checkland's departure in March 1993. I would like to think that if I had been on the Board at the material time I would have argued against an arrangement virtually bound to end in tears. Checkland had made it known that he did not intend to be a mere caretaker for his truncated second period in office. Yet the Corporation needed strong and unambiguous leadership at a difficult and critical time. It was becoming clear that even those currently in government who were broadly supportive of the BBC in principle regarded it as wasteful, over-manned and over-ambitious in practice. Staff reductions, causing the usual upset and uncertainty, were well under way, but Checkland was coming under pressure to up the pace. Building on the work of the task forces, the case for Charter renewal on acceptable terms had to be developed. Meanwhile Birt was demonstrating that enthusiasm for consultancy advice and business school methods which, unsurprisingly, was to win him after leaving the BBC an appointment as an adviser to McKinsey's global media practice; a sort of consultant to the consultants. Quite early on Hussey, who had been disappointed not to secure the immediate promotion of Birt, nevertheless began to show some signs of nervousness about the extent and growing cost of consultancy advice. All of this activity would build up to the publication in November 1992 of 'Extending Choice', followed in April 1993 by the launch of Birt's 'big idea', Producer Choice.

These potentially troubled waters were stirred up in January 1992 by an intervention from the former Director General, Alasdair Milne, whose disagreeable experience of having his BBC career rather brutally cut short had hardly pre-disposed him to refrain from criticism of the current running of the Corporation. In the course of a *Guardian* article he had not minced his words: 'The governors have forced out one Director General, handed down a contemptuous offer of a year's extension to another, and appointed a third without advertisement, competition or even formal interview. They appear to exalt administration and management above creative leadership.'

In May 1992 I would be involved for the first time in the annual conference of the Boards of Governors and Management. In the atmosphere of growing political pressure about 'BBC extravagance' it was a totally crazy decision to hold this conference in the lush and ritzy surroundings of Lucknam Park, a luxury hotel near Bath, and a suitable setting for a Jane Austen drama. One could see the merit of getting away from our regular bunker in Broadcasting House, but the

BBC itself had perfectly comfortable and entirely suitable accommodation at its own training centre, Wood Norton, which would indeed be used for our conferences on later occasions. As it was, Lucknam Park was so besieged by journalists that we became virtual prisoners within its grounds. Enterprising hacks had made a point of visiting the hotel in advance, ordering its most fancy and expensive dishes and wines, so as to extrapolate the thesis that we would be subsisting, not on locusts and wild honey but on pate de foie gras and Dom Perignon, all at the licence-payers' expense. It was an 'own goal' of colossal magnitude.

While the main purpose of the annual conference was to review progress over the previous year and set objectives for the new one, it was normal drill for the responsible Secretary of State to exchange thoughts with us on the first evening. On this occasion in 1992 it was David Mellor, as Secretary for the National Heritage. He gave us, I thought, frank views and sound advice. There were clearly colleagues in government and party who would happily rein us in, or even put us to the sword. He would be prepared to defend the BBC, but would need ammunition. This would have to take the form of clear and measurable action to tackle over-manning and extravagance. Politicians had not failed to notice how lavishly, in terms of manpower or other resources, the BBC covered events like party conferences by comparison with our commercial competitors. Declarations of good intent would not of themselves be good enough; when the crucial decisions about Charter renewal and the licence fee came to be taken, there must be reliable evidence of real movement in the right (economical) direction. Above all, the Corporation should avoid the appearance of trying to pre-empt the government by publishing its own vision of the future in advance of the anticipated government Green Paper. If the visions presented had common features, it would be better if this was seen as the Corporation's response to government proposals rather than an effort to anticipate them.

About this time concern was developing within the Board about a risk of exceeding the government-imposed borrowing limit as a result of an 'overspend' on Network Television. Some of us were left with the uncomfortable feeling that the finances of the Corporation were not fully under control, despite the leadership of a Director General from a financial background.

Meanwhile other broadcasting mandarins outside the BBC were intervening in the debate about the future direction of the Corporation; David Elstein at the Edinburgh Television Festival strongly supportive of action, led by Birt, to 'streamline' the BBC; Michael Grade, at the same venue on another occasion and reflecting his previous bad relationship with Birt as a colleague, giving dire warnings about the 'dismemberment' of the BBC by Birtist reforms.

With all this controversy breaking out around him, it was neither very surprising, nor in my view reprehensible, that Checkland's patience and self-control finally snapped. Under questioning by Jon Snow, Michael would describe the arrangements for handover to Birt (and with some justice) as 'ludicrous' and criticise Hussey's extended term in the chair as excessive. We were by now within months of the planned installation of John Birt, and in discussion a number of us decided that a further prolongation of the interregnum could only damage Checkland, Birt and the Corporation itself. It was therefore suggested to Checkland that it would be in the general interest to bring his retirement forward; and I doubt if this approach came as a surprise after his uncharacteristic outburst. So it came to pass that on 10th November 1992 Checkland announced his intention to step down towards the end of the calendar year, and on 19th December Birt realised his ambition on becoming the twelfth Director General of the BBC.

At the heart of Birt's vision was the concept called Producer Choice. No doubt aided by his consultancy advisers, John had identified within the BBC a weakness too often shared by other organisations more or less within the public sector; that the 'creative people' had become too detached from, and even oblivious of, the true costs of what they were creating. He saw the Corporation as a 'command economy' which needed to be converted into a 'trading institution'. 'Business Units' were to be established; they would have to pay an appropriate price for services bought in, whether from other units of the Corporation or from outside; and for the first time BBC producers as budget holders would have to take account of the true costs of what they planned to do. As it became clear that various services would be less expensive if bought in, there would be inevitable redundancies and the consequent adverse effect on morale. Birt would expose himself to accusations of choking the Corporation with bureaucracy and placing fetters on creativity. Yet in truth this unpopular policy would reveal a good deal of previously concealed waste and inefficiency, and enable increased spending on programmes within the revenue from a fixed licence fee. Savings achieved by 'Birtism' would not accrue to the Exchequer but to the BBC itself.

Yet this policy, which became effective from 1st April 1993, remained controversial and widely unpopular throughout Birt's tenure as DG. In his own personality he was far from being the ideal salesman of a new approach. Moreover, as originally introduced, Producer Choice created far too many Business Units and carried the transactional nature of wholly internal business to levels of grotesque absurdity.

Nevertheless Birt was to retain the loyalty of senior colleagues on the Board of Management, and to work closely with some 'true believers' inside and outside that Board. Here I would single out Margaret Salmon, a no-nonsense Personnel Director, the able John Smith (later to be Director of Finance) and Patricia Hodgson. Patricia, a former Secretary of the Corporation, was appointed by Birt to lead a high-powered new Policy and Planning Unit. She was to be unflatteringly described in an anti-Birt diatribe as 'looking like she was sculpted from deep-frozen Oil of Ulay', but for myself I found her cool rather than cold, extraordinarily able and capable of attracting other able people to work with her. In later days she would become Chief Executive of the Independent Television Commission before election to be Principal of Newnham College, Cambridge. She is today a member of the BBC Trust. Those who wrote or spoke of her in such dismissive terms seemed to conclude that any involvement in Birtist policies at the BBC was malign, stupid or both. Having met the best brains in the Home Civil and Diplomatic services, I would rate her as the intellectual equal of any of them.

However the Birt project came perilously close to being derailed only a short distance down the line. At the end of February 1993 the *Independent on Sunday* revealed to the world, and to Governors like myself who were totally unaware of it, that our Director General, Editor in Chief and Chief Executive had never become a member of the BBC staff, but essentially remained a freelance contracted through a company, John Birt Productions Ltd. The newspaper suggested that this arrangement had been made to secure for Birt certain tax advantages. The DG was photographed in an Armani suit (which, incidentally, I would have paid not to wear), with the inference that these tax advantages allowed him to offset the cost of personal clothing against tax. Over the days which followed a feeding frenzy mounted rapidly. It became clear that the Governors would have to meet to consider the future of the Director General. On Sunday 14th March the *Independent on Sunday* had carried, with my photograph, the precise terms in which I had replied to their inquiries about my attitude under the heading 'Should John Birt resign?' I had simply told them 'What I have to say I shall say to my colleagues when I meet them.' The *Mail on Sunday* was, very typically, less cautious and more imaginative. Under a heading 'The way Governors line up in the controversy over the DG's tax bill' appeared photographs of the twelve members of the Board. Duke Hussey, Lord Barnett, Lord Nicholas Gordon-Lennox, Baroness James, Jane Glover, Shahwar Sadeque and I were listed as 'for keeping Birt' while Sir Graham Hills, John Roberts, Gwyn Jones, Bill Jordan and Keith Oates were described as 'against keeping Birt'. I can only suppose that this miraculous revelation of my opinion had been achieved by reading tea-leaves or other arcane modes of divination, since I had not expressed a view to that paper or to anyone else. One does not have to be a lawyer to appreciate that it is wise to hear the evidence before reaching a judgement.

However, throughout this critical period I received an extraordinary number of calls from senior BBC staff, not all of whom would have been regarded as friends or fans of John Birt, pleading that the Board should not plunge the Corporation into further uncertainty just as a new regime was gathering momentum and at a critical time for the BBC. I received a similar message from some very well-known people outside the Corporation.

Duke Hussey's absence abroad at this critical time meant that we could not hold the crucial Board meeting until the eve of St Patrick's Day. This placed me personally in a hideously embarrassing situation. On a day celebrated by the Irish diaspora around the world, my wife and I had accepted separate invitations to perform at events far from home. Liz would fly out to Hong Kong, her luggage improbably laden with potato bread, soda farls and other local delicacies, to speak at a lunch in the Hong Kong Cricket Club held to raise funds for Bryson House, a leading Belfast charity. I, on the other hand, had accepted an invitation to fly off in the opposite direction, to Toronto in Canada, for a huge St Patrick's Day event at which I would be a principal guest speaker alongside an Irish cabinet minister. With real embarrassment and regret, I decided that my BBC duties must take precedence. I then had to phone my Canadian hosts, explain the situation and ask that my prepared text should be read out.

While I appreciated the clear wish of so many people to avoid an upset at the summit of the Corporation, I went to the crucial meeting determined not to make my mind up until every aspect of the situation had been clarified and explored. In the course of the meeting a number of things became clear to me. The first was that a considerable number of prominent broadcasting people, like managers of football teams, anticipated the possibility of movement from one employer to another. Just as many of those we saw in front of a BBC camera were not on the BBC staff, so it was not unprecedented for producers or managers to 'hire out' their talents and services for the time being. The arrangements made with John Birt on joining the BBC had been similar to those agreed in the past for some other senior managers. Yet the 'optics' of the Chief Executive not being a member of the staff he led were bound to be very bad. Birt would have shown better judgement and more sensitivity if he had moved to regularise the position on becoming Director General. But if there was blame here, it was to be shared with those senior members of the Board who had been aware of the position and taken no initiative to change it. There were, after all, two sides to any contractual arrangement. It would be unjust to single out one contracting party for a draconian sanction. Most, though not all, of my Board colleagues shared this view. There never seemed to be any substance in allegations of tax irregularities.

Yet this unfortunate episode did claim an important casualty. For many years the BBC had maintained a large forum, the General Advisory Council (GAC), drawn from all parts of the United Kingdom, with whom Governors and management could engage in useful dialogue about the development and standards of our services. At this time the Chairman was a former civil service colleague, Sir Terence Heiser, until 1992 a legendary Permanent Secretary at the Department of the Environment. Probably unwisely, the Council decided to mount an inquest on the 'Armanigate' affair. As the meeting began, Heiser asked the BBC Governors present (including the Chairman) to withdraw. Kept waiting outside 'the headmaster's study' as it were, one could see resentment and fury mounting on the countenance of Duke Hussey who was, at the conclusion of the Council's debate, asked to 'consider his position'. Hussey felt strongly that the GAC were invading territory which was the preserve of the Governors, and decided that he would 'consider the position' of the GAC itself. Having done so, he concluded that we could do without it.

It was, in my own view, a pity. John Birt had made an error of judgement in not appreciating the 'optics' of his employment status; Hussey had made an error of judgement in not identifying this issue as one with the potential for acute embarrassment; the GAC had made an error of judgement in trying to set itself up as some kind of 'court of appeal'. Yet the members of the GAC included many who wanted to be friends and allies of the BBC, and – if critics – to be candid and constructive critics. The irony was that to me would fall the task of leading a review of the entire extensive advisory network of the BBC. It was to be one of five special roles I would undertake during my governorship, and in the next chapter I shall discuss each of these.

5

PERSONAL EXPERIENCES OF A GOVERNOR

Between my appointment in 1991 and my departure in 1999 I was involved in all the activities shared by other members of the Board: attending Board meetings and conferences, speaking to local or national media about our affairs, and taking part in public meetings not just in my own 'patch' of Northern Ireland but around the country. It was important, I concluded, for a National Governor not to be classified as a 'special interest' person, harping on endlessly about the problems and opportunities of his own base.

Public meetings were highly informative and sometimes diverting. I was intrigued to be asked to sit on a panel in Darlington, because many years before it had been the venue for one of the many conferences about the future of Northern Ireland under the chairmanship of the admirable William Whitelaw. We heard a great deal that evening, I remember, about an area called Swaledale which had not previously entered my geographical consciousness. There were problems, it seemed, about reception in that area; and indeed public meetings generally revealed that few things more agitated our licence-payers than an inability to receive a decent quality of sound and/or vision.

Often, to give a thrill to the audience, the subfusc Governors and senior managers on such panels would be chaired by some well-known and instantly recognisable television personality. In Derry, on my own home ground, the charming and courteous moderator of the evening would later transform herself into the fearsome dominatrix of *The Weakest Link*. At our first public meeting in republican West Belfast after the 1994 IRA ceasefire, Pat Loughrey, by then the Controller, and

I passed pickets at the door protesting about the dearth, as they saw it, of Irish language programmes. We sent out a message to them to emphasise that our sole purpose was to hear the views of local people, and to suggest that they might better do this by coming into the meeting and having their say, rather than standing outside with placards. They then came in and made their protest, in Irish of course. Pat, a County Donegal man, may well have understood some or all of what they said. I understood not a single word, but in any event they were totally uninterested in dialogue and abandoned the meeting, which turned to more mundane matters.

I have emphasised that I did not wish to be pigeon-holed in London as little more than a broadcasting ambassador for Northern Ireland. I did, though, take every opportunity to argue for my region to have a decent share of network television production and for the location in Northern Ireland of some element of the service infrastructure of the BBC. I knew Wales had benefited from the presence in Cardiff of the wages and salaries apparatus of the Corporation. The BBC's main activities in Wales were located at Llandaff, with which I felt a certain affinity since my father had been a chorister there in its famous cathedral during the first decade of the twentieth century. My regular pressure for locating in Northern Ireland a share of BBC-wide business led in time to the establishment of a major complaints centre at Blackstaff House in Belfast.

In my own jurisdiction I acted as Chairman of the Broadcasting Council. Since the province was long (and possibly rightly) regarded as a singularly tricky place, it had not initially been endowed with a full Broadcasting Council on a par with those in Scotland and Wales. In a society with all too manifest divisions, it was peculiarly important that the Broadcasting Council for Northern Ireland (BCNI) should be seen to be as broadly representative as possible, rather than a creature of the National Governor or of local management. The ideal Council would embrace catholic and protestant, town and country, male and female. When I arrived on the scene, a critical role in selection was played by the Northern Ireland members of the GAC, people of substance like Maurice Hayes, Mary Clark-Glass and Maurna Crozier. After exchanges about possible appointees, I would often invite credible candidates to join myself and the panel members for lunch at Broadcasting House in Belfast. The invitees would be told that, from time to time, we liked to chat to representative members of the public about how the BBC was perceived. In reality we were 'talent spotting'. Not all of those we invited were appointed soon afterwards, or at all. There might not be early vacancies, and essentially we wanted to build up a 'talent bank' from which we might draw when filling individual slots. I can recall one of our guests at such a 'getting to know you' lunch being Rhonda Paisley, a daughter of the fiery politico-cleric and future First Minister. As it happens she never joined the Council, but I remember taking away a distinct impression of a person with a mind and will of her own, deeply influenced by a powerful and loving father but capable of thinking and speaking for herself. Of course the invaluable Rosemary Kelly, acting as secretary to BCNI, would sit in on all these discussions and encounters.

I think we did a pretty decent job of shaping the Council over the years to reflect the diversity of Northern Ireland. As I have already said, my first Council included in Mary McAleese a future President of Ireland; later members included Chitra Bharucha, the Indian-educated haematologist who went on to serve from 2001 to 2003 on the Independent Television Commission and temporarily chaired the BBC Trust (successor to the Governors) following the departure of Michael Grade, and also the splendid Mark Adair, who would later be considered as a successor to myself as Governor before becoming a member of the senior management in Belfast.

We were, indeed, extraordinarily fortunate to be able to persuade so many busy and able people to devote time and effort to the BBC on a wholly unpaid basis. They would include during my time such high-flyers as Jonathan Bardon, author of a most distinguished and enjoyably readable history of Ulster; Anne Tannahill, presiding genius of the remarkable local publisher, Blackstaff Press; Pat McCartan, a respected trade union figure who went on to hold various academic and public positions; Roisin McDonough, now Chief Executive of the Arts Council; Professor Desmond Rea, now chairman of the Policing Board; Lyn Gallagher, a freelance author of great talent; Gery McGinn, at that time the head of the Bank of Ireland's operations in Northern

Ireland and later a civil service Permanent Secretary; Norma Dawson, a highly rated Professor of Law; Norman Shaw, a major figure in local and national agriculture; Ken O'Neill, a Professor of Entrepreneurship and Small Business Development, and many other articulate and experienced individuals. It said a great deal about the standing and reputation of the BBC at that time that people of this quality were ready and eager to serve it.

I am happy to say that no one in my time ever accused the BCNI of lacking balance. On the gender front, for instance, women consistently occupied about half the places. What I found particularly gratifying was that the Council never, in my eight years of experience, broke up into camps or cabals. Regardless of political or religious background, Council members seemed determined to come to the table without baggage and ready to look at issues on their merits.

I suppose that any outside observer, aware of the conflict bedevilling Northern Ireland, would have assumed that BCNI would be much more difficult to manage and keep together than its Scottish or Welsh equivalent. This did not prove to be the case. We did not have to face anything like the *Real Lives* controversy during my time in office. Perhaps people in our community, in spite of indications to the contrary, were becoming less touchy. Whether this was a product of growing tolerance or of simple weariness is an open question. Nevertheless I experienced this change of attitude in an episode not involving the BBC.

I had come to know, not intimately but on a friendly basis, the famous British film-maker David Puttnam, and had indeed persuaded him to come to Belfast to exchange ideas with local people who had aspirations to build up a local centre for cinema and television production. One day, out of the blue, Puttnam telephoned me at home about the Hollywood movie based on the life of Michael Collins and now awaiting release. I had a tenuous link with Liam Neeson, who had been cast in the starring role of the celebrated revolutionary. Neeson had cut his teeth as a professional actor at the Lyric Players Theatre in Belfast, while I had been a performer in the 1950s in the amateur company of the Lyric Players, the brain-child of the charismatic Mary O'Malley, from which it had sprung. I had played, amongst other parts, that of Horatio in *Hamlet*. Lovers of that great play will recall that in the final scene there is much mayhem; and so tiny was the stage of the bijou theatre at the back of the O'Malleys' suburban house that I found myself playing undertaker as well as courtier, to avoid a messy overlapping of corpses from the Royal Danish court. Horatio emerges as a kind of Permanent Secretary figure, so perhaps I was predestined to play him (although, being an Anglican rather than a Presbyterian, predestination does not feature prominently in my mind-set).

In his telephone call Puttnam explained that, since he was conscious of the sensitivity of the situation in Northern Ireland, he would welcome an entirely personal and informal view from me as to whether the screening of this film – with its vivid images of bloodshed and revolutionary conflict – in Northern Ireland could have an adverse impact on efforts to bridge differences. Would I, he asked, be willing to come over to London, view a private screening of the picture, and let him have my frank opinion? Intrigued by the whole affair, I agreed to do so.

I duly turned up at a small private cinema in the Wardour Street area, where I was asked if I would mind sharing the screening with another, a senior figure from the Venice Film Festival. I was, of course, quite happy to do this. Shortly afterwards we were joined by a vivacious Italian lady who explained that, as her boss's English was not perfect, she would mutter into his ear such translation as proved to be necessary. 'Have you,' she asked, 'seen the script?' (pronounced 'screept'). 'No. I have not had that opportunity.' 'You see, I am not sure I have understood all these expressions', and at that she pointed out to me (and I have now forgotten the exact words) some vernacular Irish usage such as 'Get outa the way, you gobshite.'

At last the Venetian impresario arrived, the theatre darkened, the screening began and the credits rolled. After a very few moments the Venetian rose from his seat a couple of rows ahead of me, waved his hands in the air (projecting shadows across the screen) and shouted authoritatively 'Shtop. Shtop!' I was fearful for a moment of early angina or the presence of a rat in the auditorium, but it transpired that the issue was the volume of the sound-track, making it impossible for him to hear the muffled translation.

This episode brought to my mind an incident on my first visit to

America, when I attended in Washington the meetings of the World Bank and International Monetary Fund in 1959. There I found myself seated one day close to the famed Dr Ludwig Erhard, acknowledged architect of the German 'economic miracle'. In those days before smokers became notorious health threats or social pariahs, he sat impassively with a large cigar protruding from his fleshy face, rejecting the earphones provided for translation in favour of the services of a rather glamorous female interpreter muttering into his ear such sweet nothings as 'the inexorable rise of world commodity prices' or 'inflationary pressures bearing in particular upon marginal economies', with other gobbledegook sounding even more polysyllabic in German.

At any rate *Michael Collins* was re-wound and started up again at a lower rate of decibels. I watched it with a mixture of admiration and revulsion. Scenes of bloody conflict were portrayed with great effectiveness and impact. Violence was depicted in all its banal ugliness. Some protagonists, I felt, were presented as rather crude stereotypes, while the mandatory 'love interest' verged upon the embarrassing. Although it was no surprise to find 'the Brits' portrayed in a pretty unflattering and unsympathetic way it seemed to me that the most damaging screen portrait was that of De Valera, acted as he was by the admirable Alan Rickman, who has majored on the portrayal of unlikeable or even sinister figures on British television. He had, for example, enacted a memorably horrible Mr Slope in Trollope's masterpiece.

In the end my feeling, as I expressed it to Puttnam, was that there might well be some criticism of the film if screened in Northern Ireland but hardly such as to disturb political development or provoke violence. In the event, the fascinating outcome was that the reaction in Northern Ireland was even more muted than I would have expected. Perhaps the horrible and bloody decades had de-sensitised our people to the portrayal of graphic violence. When one had seen on television after 'Bloody Friday' in Belfast pieces of human bodies being scraped up and bagged, a fictional conflict – however graphic and however true or untrue to historic reality – was likely to have a lesser impact. In any case, over the years movies generally had become increasingly graphic in the depiction of violence. People in Northern Ireland, it seemed, were now more likely to protest about Sunday opening or a

local sex-shop selling vibrators than about the incineration, eviscera-
tion or atomisation of real human beings.

At any rate BCNI was never, throughout my time, a conflict zone
as between 'the two traditions'. Perhaps the very reasonableness of
colleagues pointed to a certain failure to reflect all the harsh realities of
division and conflict within Broadcasting House.

In outlining the role and practices of the Board of Governors
I have made clear my antipathy to the pre-viewing of programmes
and my scepticism about the post-broadcast value of purely personal
opinions about programmes directed to audiences of very different
backgrounds. On the other hand it was the practice at BCNI, at each of
its monthly meetings, to ask members to watch or listen to if possible
a limited number of the programmes made for local consumption.
These varied expressions of opinion from members of a broadly-
based Council were, I know, valued by management, and could be set
alongside excellent hard data on audience numbers and audience appreciation presented to us by Peter Johnston, clearly a potential 'high-flyer'
and today the Regional Controller in Belfast.

Just as the work of the Board was brought into sharp annual focus
at the joint conference of the Boards of Governors and management,
so the BCNI year would reach its conclusion at an 'away weekend'
held in some quiet and salubrious bolthole like the Radisson Hotel in
Limavady. Here the Council would review performance during the past
year and set broad objectives for the year ahead. Sometimes, to inspire
us, we would invite a distinguished guest to join us for dinner, and we
might well be joined also by the member of the Board of Management
responsible for regional broadcasting. In my earliest days I worried
about the rather tenuous links between National Broadcasting Councils
and the Board. While their several sets of minutes were made available
to Governors, these could too easily be buried under the mountains
of paper supporting the Board agenda. I shall explain later how work
on the Corporation's advisory machinery, which I led, would produce
the welcome outcome of direct annual access by each Broadcasting
Council to the full Board.

It is interesting to look back now to the forewords which, as
National Governor, I would contribute to the Annual Review of BBC

Northern Ireland published for the first time in 1995. In my first contribution I explained to readers that Northern Ireland, like Scotland and Wales, enjoyed a special status within the BBC as a 'national region'. Under the Charter then coming to the end of its life, there was provision for each such national region to have a National Broadcasting Council 'to control the policy and content of BBC radio and television programmes produced primarily for its region, and taking into account the culture, language, interests and tastes of the people who live there'. Use of the word 'control' was a significant indication that, in the last resort, Council powers extended well beyond the purely advisory. In most circumstances the Council and local management would work together, but in the last resort the Council could put its foot down.

A government White Paper, 'The Future of the BBC', published in July 1994, strongly endorsed a continuing role for the Broadcasting Councils under the new Charter which was to run from 1996. The Government saw it as the first responsibility of BCNI and its counterparts to represent the views and interests of local people to the Board of Governors and the Corporation's senior managers. The Broadcasting Councils should have a particular responsibility for keeping in touch with audiences and ensuring that any comments, proposals or complaints from them were handled satisfactorily. They should be in a position to assess whether or not the BBC was achieving its dual aims of reflecting the views and interests of Northern Ireland in its programmes, and of ensuring that Northern Ireland had an opportunity to make a reasonable contribution to national output. In 1994 the Board had taken a very significant decision to shift the emphasis in programme making to the broad benefit of national and other regions. However, it would require demonstrable excellence for a specific region to benefit from these new opportunities. No individual region was guaranteed a specific 'share' of network production; those commissioning for BBC1 and BBC2 television were interested only in programmes which could win a place in their schedules on merit. The new policy, advocated by David Hatch, offered to each region not a guarantee but an opportunity. It was, therefore, gratifying to record an increase of 230 per cent over the previous year in network television commissions won by BBC Northern Ireland. It has to be appreciated, though, that not every programme commissioned from BBC Northern Ireland and carrying its logo would be made by the BBC rather than an independent, nor would all the benefits of such a commission necessarily accrue within the region. With attractive tax benefits on offer, it was not surprising to find *Ballykissangel*, for example, filmed in the Irish Republic.

1994, of course, had been the year of the initial IRA ceasefire, and the lifting after six years of the 'broadcasting ban'. In its review the Broadcasting Council welcomed 'the return to a clear and unimpeded role for the BBC as the balanced reporter of events in Northern Ireland, both within the Region and on the Networks'.

Successive Reviews during my time caused me to reflect on the professional reaction of local broadcasters to the challenge of striking events: the extraordinary visit of President Clinton to Belfast and Derry in November 1995; the subsequent sad breach of the ceasefire at Canary Wharf in February 1996; the Oscar nomination for a short film made in Northern Ireland; the dreadful Omagh atrocity and its aftermath; the development of regional Ceefax and the implications of digital technology. In my final Foreword to the 1989/99 Review I was proud to commend the production of a remarkable CD ROM 'A State Apart'. Through its imaginative use of leading edge multi-media technology, this project assembled an extraordinary resource for students and scholars, an incomparable testimony to our time of trial. And, since it had been what I described as 'a painful privilege' to serve as Victims Commissioner for Northern Ireland and produce in 1998 the report *We Will Remember Them*, it was wonderfully imaginative of the BBC to broadcast, morning after morning through the year, brief but telling personal accounts from many very different people affected by 'the Troubles'.

I have earlier made the point that, through the most difficult and trying times, the BCNI remained remarkably united and uniformly responsible. My Scottish and Welsh colleagues did not always have such an easy ride. In Scotland in particular my good friend Revd Norman Drummond faced a task of great sensitivity as Council Chairman and National Governor. Norman was at all times a splendid ally and a true good guy. More than twenty years younger than myself, he had packed an enormous amount into his life before he joined our Board in 1994.

A Cambridge graduate, former rugby footballer of near-international standard, a parachute padre and a headmaster of the famous Loretto School in his early thirties, Norman had abundant charm, eloquence and integrity. At his home on the rugged Isle of Skye he acted as a parish minister in the Church of Scotland. At his invitation I had attended a meeting of the Scottish Broadcasting Council at Stornoway on the Isle of Lewis and visited Skye itself shortly before the new bridge replaced the ferry as a connection with mainland Scotland.

Whenever I could I made a point of attending the annual Celtic Film and Television Festival at such locations as Derry in Northern Ireland, Bangor in North Wales or Portree on the Isle of Skye. These were strange and stimulating syntheses of culture and whisky (or, for those who preferred it, whiskey). On occasions delegates would come from the wilder shores of Celtic nationalism. In Derry, for example, where I chaired a talk by David Glencross of the Independent Television Commission and thereafter invited questions or comments, I had to cope with the firm affirmation that 'the first duty of a broadcaster is to bring down the state'. At the conclusion of the event in Portree, a Scots 'minder' introduced me to the local pub. All was harmonious until we were joined by a posse of very fervent Breton nationalists, who had attended primarily to demonstrate their antipathy to all things French. 'You're French, then?', innocently enquired a local. Mayhem then ensued. I suspect the Portree locals might have reacted similarly if asked in Brittany 'You're English, then?'

The position of the BBC in relation to Scotland was bound to be affected by the onset of devolution and the growth of Scots nationalism. Under devolution broadcasting would remain a subject reserved to Westminster (as in Northern Ireland) but the Scots did not want to be sealed off from the impact of such a powerful media instrument. In London producers were not always sufficiently alert to the fact that events hitherto commonly described as 'national' were now essentially 'English'. The issue would come to a head over pressures for a 'Scottish Six'. This arose from the widespread view in Scotland that local broadcasters would be perfectly capable of providing in and for Scotland a main television news bulletin of the day covering international, UK and Scottish affairs. No one could doubt that BBC Scotland, now led as Controller by the admirable and immensely experienced John McCormick, would be perfectly competent to manage this. Yet it infringed on a deeply entrenched view that the concept of 'one BBC' should not be breached; that an important part of the cement holding the UK together was the opportunity for families across the nation to share a common broadcasting experience. While I was on most issues a natural ally of Norman Drummond and BBC Scotland, I was no more than lukewarm, for various reasons, about the concept of a 'Scottish Six'. The majority of the Board were antipathetic to Scotland's claim. The unfortunate Will Wyatt and Tony Hall, two of the best and brightest from the Board of Management, were sent north of the Border for an uncomfortable confrontation with the Scottish Council and given a very hot time. It was, I think, unfortunate that over time the practice had developed of designating a specific Vice Chairman of the Scottish Council. I was careful not to follow that example, simply nominating a senior BCNI colleague to stand in for me if I was unable to attend a particular meeting. In a difficult situation the Scottish Governor could find himself torn in two directions, and possibly confronting a faction led by his deputy. While the 'Scottish Six' as such was not conceded, one useful outcome for all the regions was a much more seamless transition from the national segment of the evening news to the regional segment. Careful use of technology, music and symbols made 'And now over to our news team where you are' as natural as 'And now over to Kabul'.

I have made the point that the Broadcasting Councils had a role and function well beyond the purely advisory. Nevertheless they formed one element of a large, complex, elaborate and expensive network of advisory and consultative bodies sponsored and supported by the BBC. In 1993 I was commissioned by my colleagues to chair a group to review this network and make recommendations, where necessary, for its re-shaping or improvement. My committee for the purpose would include experienced BBC managers and in particular the reliable and wise Ron Neil. I have earlier described the unhappy fate of the 'top tier' of our advisory structure, the General Advisory Council, when it had tried the not unlimited patience of Duke Hussey.

The pursuit of this wide-ranging remit unearthed some fundamental questions and produced some intriguing encounters. To whom, precisely, were a particular group offering advice? The Board of Governors or the professional programme makers? If the latter, was it sensible to entrench any group of individuals as privileged advisers over a term of years, rather than afford the opportunity to turn to sources of advice relevant to a specific programme or programmes? I had begun to appreciate that the expectation of 'balance' from the BBC over the whole range of its programmes could lead to some absurd consequences. I had, as it happened, been commissioned by the Government to conduct an inquiry into the knotty problem of the pay of dentists under the NHS. (I am not sure whether the present perilous of the General Dental Service is to be attributed to my report, or to the procrastination of successive governments in reacting to my disturbing conclusions.) One could not enter such a subject without encountering the issue of fluoridation of the water supply as a means to inhibit dental decay. Scientific advice on this subject was split, as it often is. On one side a huge majority of knowledgeable scientists supported fluoridation as a real net health benefit; on the other side a relatively small minority saw in the procedure unacceptable health risks. In instances like this, the BBC would sometimes feel obliged to present 'both sides of the argument' as if the respective champions had equal weight in the scientific community. As I write this, I have in mind a very recent local programme in which a broadcaster of great experience and common sense interviewed the declared atheist Professor Dawkins of Oxford University. (Improbably the setting for this onslaught on any and all religions was the chapel of my old college.) What, if any, part should a Dawkins play on CRAC (not a banned substance but the Central Religious Advisory Council established to advise both the BBC and ITV on religious broadcasting)? Should 'religious broadcasting', in a country increasingly indifferent to organised religion, include irreligious or even anti-religious voices?

I found it helpful to meet some of the principal figures. The current chairman of CRAC, Roy Williamson, then Bishop of Southwark, proved to be a native Ulsterman who had attended as a boy the Belfast church in which I had been confirmed, St Donard's in the Bloomfield district of Belfast. The distinguished Chairman of our Scientific Advisory Council, a future President of the Royal Society, arrived for a breakfast meeting at the Langham Hotel still wearing his bicycle clips.

In all of this there was no challenge to Broadcasting Councils as a requirement of the Charter. Indeed, as we considered their prescribed role and function two things became clear. First, that while Scotland, Wales and Northern Ireland had guaranteed access to the Board table, there was no one charged with the responsibility of speaking for the distinctive English regions which also produced programmes for local as well as network consumption. We therefore argued the case for an 'English National Governor', who would initially have to be allocated that role by internal decision of the Board itself, but hopefully would in time occupy a position entrenched by Charter.

Secondly, it did not seem good enough that the contact between Broadcasting Councils and the Board rested solely upon issues raised by the specific National Governor or set out in minutes often given no more than a passing glance by busy colleagues. So it was that we recommended an annual encounter between the whole Board and a delegation from each of the Councils (and from non-network England). This initiative would give real meaning and focus to the work of the Councils themselves. They would have to think carefully about what arguments to produce within limited time, and which of their members should present them. Watching the system later in operation, I could see how seriously BCNI members took this responsibility; how they refined and rehearsed their arguments; how well the local secretary, Rosemary Kelly, supported them.

As for the idea of an 'English National Governor', this was launched in 1994 when Margaret Spurr, a retired headteacher and a great friend, was appointed to chair an English National Forum. Margaret was more or less a contemporary of mine, and sometimes on bus journeys to provincial centres we would nostalgically re-visit in song recollections of our earlier listening to BBC Radio: 'We three, from Happidrome, working for the BBC, Ramsbotham and Enoch and me'. In time her successor would be Ranjit Sondhi, an Englishman of Indian origins and a mainstay of many public bodies. He was awarded a well-earned CBE in an Honours List during my last year as a Governor, and at the following Board meeting our chairman Sir Christopher Bland offered our universal congratulations. Ranjit, whose father had I believe been an important official in India, memorably replied: 'I think if my dear father were alive today, he might be surprised to find me commanding the British Empire.' A part of the advisory machinery which more than justified itself was the central Education Advisory Council and its local equivalent in Northern Ireland. Educational broadcasting was a very important support to teaching and learning, and part of the central mission of the BBC. Through the involvement of education professionals in our advisory arrangements, we could ensure continuing relevance to curricular demands. As I have pointed out, not a few eminent BBC figures had joined the Corporation after a career in teaching.

Some advisory bodies were subsequently stood down to encourage access by production staff to currently relevant advice, but the main useful outcome was a better articulation between the centre of the BBC and its several nations and regions.

For reasons I no longer remember, a deadline had been set for the presentation of our report. In April 1993 I was enjoying a short holiday with my family on the Spanish coast close to Gibraltar. I remember I had to fly back to London for a busy day to finalise our report before returning to Spain. There has always been speculation that a covey of monkeys randomly typing indefinitely would eventually replicate the works of Shakespeare. I would wish to disavow any suggestion that our report on the advisory bodies bore the imprint of the Barbary apes on the Rock.

I was to be concerned also with fundamental questions of governance and accountability. The precise powers and responsibilities of the Governors had so far been defined in relatively vague terms. In 1997 my colleague Lord Nicholas Gordon-Lennox and I took the lead in developing with the Secretary an updated 'code' for our governance, published as 'Governing Today's BBC: Broadcasting, the Public Interest and Accountability'.

Nicky and I worked particularly well as a team. On the one hand we had similar professional backgrounds as career bureaucrats, in his case as a member of the Diplomatic Service, rising to the rank of Ambassador. We were used to working with complex organisations and framing our conclusions in clear and concise language. On the other hand, his social background was very different from my own. I was the product of a modest upbringing, elementary and grammar schools, with a 'topping up' at Oxford; he the son of a ducal family distinguished in our history. None of these differences mattered in the least. Nicky was humorous, shrewd, and completely down to earth. Only once did I briefly glimpse the gulf between his environment and mine. We had just finished a Joint Boards Conference at Wood Norton. As my colleague got into his car, I asked 'Going home now, Nicky?' 'No. I'm off to Spain for a few days holiday with a friend. The Duke of Wellington actually.' I remember on one occasion quizzing him about the famous ball held by his ancestor on the eve of the Battle of Waterloo. 'More of a hop, really', he said.

After we had both left the Corporation, he died too young. I look back on my experience of working with him with tremendous pleasure. Our conclusions, embodied at greater length in the published 'code', were well summarised in the Governors' contribution to the Corporation's 1997/98 Report.

> The Governors of the BBC are appointed by the Crown as trustees for the public interest. The Board of Governors ensures that the BBC is appropriately accountable to Parliament, licence payers and the viewers and listeners. Our role is to determine overall strategy and objectives, to assess the BBC's performance and to keep in touch with what viewers and listeners are telling us about BBC services. We ensure that the BBC complies with its Royal Charter and laws and regulations governing broadcasting, and that programme makers observe the guidelines which we authorise.

The use of the term 'trustees for the public interest' had been adopted long before by my college contemporary Colin Shaw. I must confess that when the present government decided to replace the Board of Governors with a BBC Trust I reflected that we had viewed ourselves as a trust all along. The real issue was whether the public interest would be better served by Governors alongside management than by Trustees detached from them. I shall return to that question.

Reference to 'guidelines' was significant. It is an extraordinary fact that, as the senior local permanent official in Northern Ireland, I had joined the BBC unaware of, and uninformed about, the existence in guidelines of extensive advice relating specifically to Northern Ireland. The place in those days was a semantic minefield. Whether one referred to 'Derry' or 'Londonderry'; whether one referred to 'Northern Ireland' or 'the six counties' or 'the north of Ireland'; whether one referred to 'the Army', 'the British Army' or 'our Army': nuances such as these were monitored to an obsessive extent. Prudently the Corporation had given extensive and well-considered guidance to the makers of all programmes touching on Northern Ireland, including the advisability of consultation with local management. Such carefulness, replicated in many other sensitive areas, should have been a reassurance to all. But if I, close as I was to the centre of our politics and administration, did not know of this, who else did? Without this reassuring knowledge we were like football spectators unaware of the offside rules or rugby fans ignorant of the implications of the forward pass.

Overall the well-considered and regularly reviewed guidelines provided sage advice over an extremely wide range of sensitive and potentially controversial issues. Periodically the Governors would meet to consider whether the letter and spirit of their guidelines had been observed or needed to be modified. The object was not to deliver or imply censure for honest misjudgements but to give clarifying guidance for the future. We could find ourselves considering issues like covert filming to expose wrongdoing, including deception about the identity of investigative journalists. An issue I personally addressed more than once was the need for great care in screening 'faction', that is to say a purported reconstruction of real events, using actors to portray real (and living) personalities. Even in the case of a televised presentation of an inquiry or trial, with actors using only words from a formal transcript, an impression – which might be fair or unfair – could be created by the demeanour and tone of voice adopted by an actor. Oddly enough, I had seen precisely this point effectively made in a television programme years before. It had related to a famous trial in which Sir Francis Camps, the celebrated Home Office pathologist of the time, had appeared for the prosecution and another well-qualified, but less well-known pathologist for the defence. In terms of dispassionate print the presiding judge, in his summing up, had seemed to hold a reasonably fair balance. 'On the one hand, you have listened to the evidence of Professor Camps, the eminent Home Office pathologist. As against this you will have to weigh the evidence of Professor Blank.' As acted, however, the stress placed by the presiding judge on the word 'eminent', and a faint trace of a sneer as he referred to 'the evidence of Professor Blank' seemed to be giving a subtle nudge to the jury.

This area was of particular interest and concern to me because so many of the most controversial events of our time had, unhappily, occurred in Northern Ireland. Thus I would see from time to time on one channel or another actors portraying such people as the former RUC Chief Constables, Sir John Hermon and Sir Ronnie Flanagan, both of whom I knew well. I watched with particular interest a reconstruction of the appalling Omagh bomb and its aftermath. Real and entirely valid questions have been asked, by the Police Ombudsman and others, about the police handling of these events, but the unsympathetic, cold and uncaring Flanagan portrayed on the screen bore no resemblance at all to a man I knew well. It is surprising, is it not, that if he had resembled in any way the man portrayed on the screen, he was chosen subsequently to be the Chief Inspector of Constabulary and the chief professional policing adviser to the Home Secretary?

Throughout the 1990s, growing emphasis was being placed, across both the public and private sectors, on issues of corporate governance. In this context it became an embarrassment that the BBC had not yet established an Audit Committee. When the decision was rather belatedly taken to establish such a Committee, there was an ideal chairman to hand in the person of our Vice Chairman, Joel Barnett. As a former Treasury minister, onetime chairman of the PAC and a professional accountant Joel was the obvious person to take on this important role. Small, shrewd and incisive, Barnett had put the fear of God into me and other Accounting Officers of the civil service.

However, one could not establish a one-man Audit Committee, and so the chairman, Duke Hussey, had to persuade others to serve. Here I have to insert an honest confession. All my life I have been a 'words man' rather than a 'figures man'. In school examinations I could exhibit some degree of distinction in English, history and languages. In mathematics I rivalled Jacques Cousteau in plumbing hitherto undiscovered depths. I suppose the nadir of my performance was 17 per cent in geometry, but neither in arithmetic nor algebra did I emerge as a potential Nobel prize-winner. At Oxford I had read history, history and more history, with modest excursions into historical geography (the voyages of Vasco da Gama) or Latin (in the incredibly tedious effusions of the Venerable Bede). I am afraid raucous undergraduates made mockery of this saintly man and primitive historian in the imaginary dialogue:

'Who's the venereal old gentleman in the gold-rimmed testicles?'
'That's our new rectum. Have you not been seduced to him yet?'

Such was the high tone of undergraduate wit in the early 1950s!

Thereafter I entered the civil service on the basis of an examination largely replicating my university studies, and requiring me to show no aptitude for number, statistics or economics. Then the service, with its unerring capacity to hammer square pegs into round holes, posted me at once to the Treasury Division of the Ministry of Finance. My kindly and indulgent first master, C. J. Bateman (later, as Sir Cecil Bateman, Head of the Civil Service) soon sensed my discomfort with figures; a fairly evident disadvantage for a Finance official. In a valiant effort to kill or cure, Cecil allocated me the task of preparing for one element of a forthcoming Northern Ireland budget. In those dim and distant days, Northern Ireland enjoyed some limited powers of local taxation, including in particular an Entertainments Tax, levied for the most part on cinema tickets. To 'police' this system we had, I recall, an inspector who would visit cinemas to detect any evasion of the duty. This would take him to insanitary and insalubrious 'picture palaces' in run-down urban areas. He would return with horrid tales of ruinous stairways; of an occasion when a patron had smuggled a live cat into the auditorium under his raincoat, swung the unfortunate animal by the tail and released it, clawing and spitting in the dark, to compete pandemonium.

At any rate Cecil Bateman set me the task of undertaking certain calculations which would assist in reaching decisions about the forward rate of duty. 'Bring me,' I said, 'last year's returns from the cinemas.' I then sat back, expecting to receive some slim summary and a few columns of accompanying statistics. Instead a 'dolly', loaded with carelessly filed individual returns from every cinema in Northern Ireland, rumbled along the Stormont corridor. Faced with the prospect of days and days of laborious calculation, I dug deep into my unhappy memory of logarithms, and to my total surprise found them of practical use.

Many years would then pass before I became the Permanent Secretary of a 'spending department'. For a small place like Northern Ireland the Department of the Environment was a huge organisation, employing more than 10,000 people and performing many of the functions undertaken elsewhere by local authorities. Unusually I had risen to the rank of Permanent Secretary with minimal previous exposure to detailed questions of financial management and control. As a Cabinet Office official I had been primarily concerned with the broad thrust of policy and the political management of the province. In those days spending departments had an Accountant (often a person with no formal accountancy qualification) who would arrive one critical and testing day to invite his Permanent Secretary to sign off the Appropriation Accounts for submission to Parliament. On each such occasion I would recall a favourite anecdote about a visit years before to the Belfast shipyards of a delegation of Soviet shipbuilders. When asked 'What do you think of this bit of machining?', a condescending Soviet apparatchik had replied 'In the Soviet Union such work must be done to the tolerance of a thousandth part of an inch'. The Harland and Wolff foreman was not to be patronised. 'Sure that's nathin'. Here we have to be dead on.'

Government departments were expected by the Comptroller and Auditor General (C&AG) and Parliament to be as close as possible to 'dead on'. Overspending of one's voted budget could lead to an Excess Vote, definitely a black mark. Underspending could in those days mean the loss for all time of resources valuable to the department and its suitors. All of this came to an annual crunch with the Appropriation Accounts. As Permanent Secretary one was also Accounting Officer, and in that capacity responsible to Parliament for the voted money and open to censure by the PAC for any misdeeds. What could one do at this juncture? Could one plod one's way through pages and pages of figures and text, probing this, that and the other? Or would it be more sensible to assure oneself of the professionalism and previous record of the Accountant, fix him with an eagle eye while saying 'I am relying on you', and append one's signature? Happily no one discovered any flaw in any Appropriation Account I signed on those terms. Inevitably, though, over the years some horror would emerge within a departmental empire (probably previously unknown to the Permanent Secretary), bringing on a report by the C&AG and the dubious pleasure of appearing at the PAC before Joel Barnett or another chairman of that august and scary body. In my own case, picking over the muddy ground of the De Lorean fiasco had been a particularly excruciating experience.

I suppose it was the assumption that a Permanent Secretary must be at home with questions of accountability that persuaded Duke Hussey to ask me to join Joel Barnett on the first Audit Committee of the BBC. Under his vigorous chairmanship I was content to play a pretty modest part; few glitches could escape his shrewd and analytical gaze. It was, however, a real surprise and even a bit of a shock when Dukie asked me to take over from Barnett when his term on the Board expired. It was only partly in jest that I protested 'You should know, Chairman, that I have never been able to count.' The reply was typical of him. 'That may be so, dear boy, but you know how this place works.' So, with a good deal of misgiving, I took on this onerous and responsible role for the rest of my time on the Board.

With colleagues at various times of much greater and more relevant experience (such as Sir David Scholey, once spoken of as a possible Governor of the Bank of England) I relied heavily on professional advice and support from three sources. There would be the Corporation's Director of Finance; up to 1998 Rodney Baker-Bates and thereafter John Smith. These were very different personalities, but each was professional and a source of excellent advice. Rodney had joined the BBC from the Midland Bank and was the quintessence of the urbane, experienced, avuncular banker of the more traditional sort; smartly and conservatively dressed, amusing and clubbable. His successor John Smith, a most able and acute accountant, would rise after my time on his transcendent merit to ever more influential positions in the Corporation, as Chief Operating Officer and Chief Executive of BBC Worldwide. John was wise, clever and tough. Oddly enough our paths would cross briefly some time after my retirement from the BBC Board. When the BBC invited bids to manage its property portfolio I was briefly engaged as a consultant by Trillium (later Land Securities Trillium). In the event Trillium completed a deal with the BBC, which ultimately failed to satisfy the expectations of the parties.

Another important arm for me was the Internal Audit capacity within the BBC, and of course a key link in the chain of control and accountability was represented by our external auditors, KPMG. Here the responsible partner was the formidable Sheila Masters, made DBE in 1996 and, since 2000, as Baroness Noakes, a Life Peer. Her portfolio also included chairing the Committee of non-executive Directors of the Bank of England since 2001. With all these sources of advice and support available to me, I could be confident of entering Audit Committee meetings well-briefed.

Of course senior members of the Board of Management, including normally the Director General, would be 'in attendance', and I must confess now that I rather enjoyed fixing John Birt, who by then had acquired a rather fearsome reputation within the Corporation, with a beady eye to ask the innocent question 'Director General, can I just have for the minutes your assurance that …?'

I remember in particular how we confronted the scary business of the 'millennium bug'. We had graphic forecasts of the chaos which might ensue as we entered the new millennium, with computers and other essential equipment immobilised, aircraft unable to land, television stations unable to transmit. Like other huge organisations heavily dependent on technology we spent many millions on protective measures. The ultimate outcome reminded me of one of my favourite sketch from *Beyond the Fringe*. In this a group of religious fanatics gather on a hillside to await the confidently predicted end of the world. A reedy voice proclaims in hieratic mode 'Now is the end; the end of the world', and begins a doom-laden countdown, 'five, four, three, two, one'. There is then a moment of absolute silence before a querulous voice disappointedly observes 'I must say it's not the spectacular conflagration I'd been expecting.' In a similar way, the world as we knew it rolled on as 1999 became 2000 without any spectacular conflagration. Did our elaborate and costly counter-measures stave off a real impending disaster? Or had we collectively summoned up a spectre to terrify ourselves?

For any Audit Committee the fulcrum event of the financial year is the meeting to consider in detail the Annual Accounts of the organisation. These would ultimately have to be signed off by the whole Board, but they in turn would rely heavily on an assurance of careful prior scrutiny by their Audit Committee. There is, of course, always a risk that members of a Board with Finance and/or Audit Committees do not sufficiently appreciate that they share ultimate responsibility for financial regularity whether or not they serve on either or both. On one memorable and nerve-wracking occasion, with the DG and other managers in attendance, a Committee colleague received disturbing news right at the start of the meeting that a close relative had been taken to hospital and understandably felt he must leave at once. Unfortunately this departure left us inquorate. I was then faced with the nightmare of a 'non-meeting', followed by frantic telephone discussion with absent members. I felt understandable uneasiness in asking the Board to sign off on my personal say-so Accounts for an expenditure in billions rather than millions. Fortunately the Finance Director and External Auditor were able to assure colleagues that there had been a thorough review of Accounts, even in these unconventional circumstances.

Chairing the Audit Committee could hardly be described as fun; that word could more readily be applied to another responsibility I had accepted in 1992; the chairmanship of the Trustees of Children in Need. Few people in the country would not watch all or part of the annual broadcast extravaganza, often featuring such curiosities as serious television journalists dancing in tutus, while performing unconventional and unprofessional ballet. Not everyone sufficiently realised that the programme, recording pledges made on the night, represented only the culmination of a vast, nationwide fundraising effort, or that the proceeds represented an absolutely indispensable lifeline for great numbers of underprivileged or disabled children in our country. In 1984 my daughter Caroline, in her last year at school, had travelled to Broadcasting House in Belfast with a classmate to present a cheque raised by her school's efforts that year, and had been thrilled to appear briefly 'on the box' in the Northern Ireland segment of the programme.

It was the responsibility of the Trust to oversee the distribution to deserving causes of the many millions of pounds raised by the annual Appeal. I use the term 'oversee' because much of the painstaking business of vetting applications and approving grants was performed by committees at a local level; in my own region, for example, by an Appeals Advisory Committee which also made recommendations on local applications from good causes to appeal 'on air'. The Board of Trustees was drawn partly from BBC management and partly from people outside the Corporation with relevant knowledge and experience. In my time this included many striking and impressive figures, including the beautiful and gifted Jane Asher – actress, novelist and the architect of wonderful cakes – and an old civil service colleague and friend in Sir Robert Andrew, formerly Permanent Under Secretary at the Northern Ireland Office and from 1989 to 1994 Director of the Esmee Fairbairn Charitable Trust. To support and advise us we had as our Chief Executive the splendid Julia Kaufmann, an acknowledged star of the charitable world.

The Chairman, of course, had the task of presiding over the periodic meetings of Trustees to review progress and, from time to time, to address tricky issues of principle. However, unlike most charitable boards of trustees, we were essentially concerned with disbursing the money rather than raising it. It was an internal BBC matter to provide the underpinning of programmes required to build up to the Appeal. The less prosaic part of the position was to act as host and front-man on the big night itself, and during my time in office from 1992 to 1998 I performed this function, normally in London at the Television Centre but once, and memorably, in my native Belfast. On that occasion I decided to remain for the local transmission because Duke Hussey, who had a soft spot for Northern Ireland, had decided to come. That tall, craggy figure could at first be intimidating to those who did not know him, but he had great reserves of charm and interest in people, and I have the clearest memory from that evening of Dukey sitting in the 'green room' enthralled by the conversation of a ferociously bohemian young man, copiously decorated with multiple tattoos and strange body ornaments.

This was at a time when, following the IRA's abortive attempt to assassinate us, my wife and I were under constant police protection and living temporarily in a 'safe house' within the grounds of Hillsborough Castle, formerly Government House and subsequently the residence of successive Secretaries of State. When I first joined the BBC, colleagues in Belfast were at first curious as to why the same two visitors were always seated in the ante-room, apparently endlessly waiting to see me. Eventually the penny dropped; these were not visitors but bodyguards. As we drove into the quiet village of Hillsborough on our way back from the Children in Need show in Belfast, one of our protective detail suddenly urged my wife to have a good look at what was happening on the right-hand side of the road. As there was patently nothing of any interest to be seen there that evening, I had a quiet word in the ear of our guardian as we returned to base. This drew a confession that, showing great initiative and presence of mind, my RUC escort had deliberately averted Elizabeth's gaze from the unexpected and unconventional sight of a young man calmly walking down one of the principal streets of that small, quiet and rather conventional village as naked as the day he was born. I discovered later that it had all been the fault of Children in Need. The television in a local pub had been screening the show and this young fellow, driven by a heady mixture of booze and benevolence, had offered to walk down the street in the buff if all his mates would pledge £5 to the appeal.

In London the focus of activity was at the Television Centre in Wood Lane. There a reception would carry on through the long evening, with opportunities for guests to go down in batches to the studio to watch the show being broadcast live. Upstairs, on the top floor of the Centre, one could encounter on such an evening an extraordinary variety of people – TV stars from soaps such as *Eastenders*, celebrities such as Steve Cram from sporting and other fields, or invitees from companies or organisations known to have raised large sums for the appeal by unconventional means. The latter included on one such occasion a group from a major British company who had called in pledges for getting their middle-aged non-climbing Chief Executive to the summit of the Matterhorn.

At some point in the evening I would be expected to make a welcoming speech. On one such occasion I found myself, quite on the spur of the moment, offering to sing. Immediately Will Wyatt, one of the truly great and dedicated BBC managers, promised £50 for the appeal if I did, and thereafter there was no turning back. When I failed to repeat my performance in subsequent years, there was an ugly rumour that someone had pledged £100 if I forebore from singing again. This I will neither confirm nor deny.

Then it would be, for Elizabeth and myself, down to the studio floor and an exchange of banter with Terry Wogan, who is exactly the same off the air or the screen as he is on it; good humoured, unstuffy, charming and friendly. I would see him at his best on another occasion at an England–Ireland game at Twickenham. In the midst of the match, spectators in the row behind us were importuning him for autographs. He could well have been forgiven for a testy reminder that he was 'off duty' and simply wanted to see the game like everyone else. But no; he had a friendly and jocular word for everyone.

I might add that my participation in another BBC-hosted party at Twickenham for the Ireland game of that season left me with a rare and improbable souvenir. The group that day were from very diverse backgrounds, and included such people as Robin Butler, David Mellor and Jeffrey Archer. Over the pre-match lunch someone suggested we have a rudimentary sweep on the result. We were all to scribble on the back of a menu card our forecast of the result. Amongst over twenty people I was the only Irishman. Not surprisingly, since England were hot favourites and Ireland not highly rated, virtually everyone else opted for an England win, in several cases by a very wide margin. Only two of the party joined me in forecasting an Ireland win, Richard Curtis (the famous progenitor of *Blackadder*, and films like *Four Weddings and a Funeral* and *Notting Hill*) and his partner Emma Freud. Sport, though, is a great lottery. Ireland have a positive genius for underperforming when strongly fancied and for triumphing when not given a chance. On this day Ireland, in this sense at least, were true to form. I could applaud the Viking-blond Simon Geoghegan (he of the most Irish name and most English accent) sprinting over for a vital try like a demented windmill. As the final minutes ticked away, Curtis beside me said 'Bloody Hell. You're not only going to win the match. You're going to win the sweep as well.' And so it proved. I scooped up my £105 of winnings and still have the menu card with its various forecasts and signatures. It gives me particular pleasure to have taken a fiver from Jeffrey Archer without rendering him any service.

6

THE GOVERNANCE OF THE BBC

By 1996 I had spent more than four years as a Governor, and had taken the opportunity to reflect on the role and functions of our Board. I was, therefore, delighted to be invited by Peter Hennessy, the doyen of contemporary British history, to speak at a London University seminar (earlier organised by A. J. P. Taylor) on the subject of BBC governance. I chose for my talk the title 'The BBC Governors: Past, Present and Future'.

I had long been interested in questions of governance in various complex public or private sector organisations. I had come to appreciate that the mere title of Governor did not of itself pin down with any great precision the nature and extent of the powers and influence to be enjoyed by its holder. One needed to look no further than the history and development of Empire and Commonwealth to appreciate that, at different times and in different situations, the Governor of a particular territory might find a place at any point along a spectrum between the exercise of near-absolute power and a constricted and largely ceremonial position.

In the case of the BBC I felt I could identify at least four sets of influences bearing upon the position of its Governors. There was, first of all, what one might call the legal framework, largely embodied in successive Royal Charters. Second, one had to consider what one might call the 'case law' of the BBC; the steady accretion of custom and practice in its governance, building up over time to well-established conventions. However, my Northern Ireland experience had made me conscious of the ultimate vulnerability of reliance on convention. It tended to represent no more and no less than what continued to seem sensible and advantageous at a particular time. Third, there would be the impact of the working environment at a particular time. Management and governance in a steady state would not necessarily be equally apt for an institution undergoing a time of crisis, under intense scrutiny or in a setting of radical change. Finally, one had to recognise the inevitable influence of powerful personalities. Anyone who has worked within a large, complex organisation will come to recognise over time that the realities of power are not always transparent on the face of the organisation chart. I still cherish the memory of an American cartoon from the 1960s. A man of powerful presence is seated at the head of an impressive table, and clustered around him are his principal associates. 'This is only a question,' he says in the caption, 'but I wouldn't like you to forget for a moment who's making it.'

To begin, then, with the formal legal framework. Since January 1927, under successive Royal Charters, the properties and powers of the British Broadcasting Corporation had been vested in its Board of Governors, who constituted the body corporate. Lord Crawford's committee of 1925 had recognised the need for a highly responsible body with an independent status to develop broadcasting in the national interest along the lines established by the British Broadcasting Company under John Reith. Since then there had been further Charters in 1937, 1947, 1952 and 1964, Supplemental Charters in 1969, 1974, 1976 and 1979, leading up to the Sixth Charter of 1981 which was due to expire at the end of 1996. Over that period of more than sixty years the successive Charters had developed an Empire Service into a World Service and taken account of the exponential development of television. However, none of the Charter additions or amendments had materially changed, or indeed defined with growing clarity, the broad constitutional role of the Governors as envisaged and established in the First Charter.

Indeed, none of the Charters had set out in any detail the working relationship between Governors and management. In an absolute sense, the Governors were the Corporation. The key provisions of the Charter as I spoke in 1994 were embodied in Articles (1) and (12). Article (1) read: 'Incorporation: The Corporation will continue to be a body corporate by the name of the British Broadcasting Corporation ... The Governors of the Corporation shall be the members thereof ...' While Article (12) read: 'Organisation: The Corporation shall appoint such officers and staff as it may from time to time consider necessary for the efficient performance of its function and transaction of its business ...'

In practice it was always accepted that there must be a sensible limit to the Governors' role. In the early years of the BBC's existence, Reith and the Governors of the day disagreed from time to time about where the limit should be set. However, in the year of my birth, 1931, Reith and the then Chairman John Whitley agreed a definition of the Governors' role in a memorandum including the key declaration that: 'The Governors of the BBC act primarily as trustees to safeguard the broadcasting service in the national interest. Their functions are not executive ...' The Whitley Memorandum was to be questioned by the Beveridge Committee reporting in 1951, followed by a Government White Paper in 1952 which took the line that the position of the Governors should be defined only by the Charter.

This, however, was really begging the question. The powers conferred by the Charter were wide, general and absolute; there could be disorder and dispute in the absence of any generally accepted and well-understood convention about their exercise in practice. On the whole the Governors continued to operate within the spirit of the Whitley Memorandum, which was subsequently updated and expanded in a 'letter to a new Governor', written by a Board member, Sir John Johnston, in 1982, approved by his colleagues and subsequently made available to new Governors on appointment.

The 'letter' included certain key phrases with an enduring resonance:

> the general government of the BBC must be by retrospective review ... they [the Governors] have made a single huge act of delega-tion, by which they have entrusted the Director General and his staff with the implementation of the purposes for which the Corporation was established ... the Board is apprehended by those working in the Corporation as the conscience of the BBC, and the ultimate guardian of its public service ethos ... the means at their disposal are primarily their power to appoint the senior staff; their power to authorise

expenditure; and what one might term their general power to call to account … we are not editors, although we are not indifferent to the editorial function. Indeed we may, on behalf of the public, have to sit in judgement on editorial decisions. We must therefore be detached from them, not a part of them … equally, we are not managers … Our concern must be with performance, and with the general efficiency of the management function we have delegated.

The Whitley Memorandum and the Johnston 'letter' might, then, be regarded as important clarifications of the custom and practice, if not the ultimate legal powers, of the Governors.

Did things always work like this in practice? Behind the carefully-crafted phrases lay the reality that the BBC was not a machine but a human institution, whose affairs were to be conducted from time to time by powerful, and on occasions mutually antipathetic, personalities. In particular, a study of the relationships over time between Chairmen and Directors General would illustrate a fascinating range of models of human behaviour. Where lines of demarcation were not absolutely clear and specific, the more assertive personality of the day might well occupy any disputed ground.

I have explained how, on joining the Board in 1991, I had been astonished by the extraordinary degree of outside media interest in all our doings. It took a little time to get used to the experience of regularly finding at the weekend apparently authoritative accounts of one's presumed, assumed or imagined position on some controversial issue, not infrequently mutually contradicting each other. It was revealing, too, to be collectively assailed both by people who alleged we were 'interfering' in every aspect of day to day work, including the editorial and programme-making responsibilities of BBC management, and by others who called on us to 'get a grip' on the organisation, usually in some wholly undefined, or at best extraordinarily ill-defined way.

My own experience indicated from the outset that there was a great deal that could and should be done without usurping the legitimate roles of the Director General and the Corporation's management. I believed it to be desirable, indeed essential, for a Governor to be visible both inside and outside the BBC; to visit BBC staff and BBC events around the country; to listen to what was being said to us by National

Broadcasting Councils and other organisations and individuals; to ensure that complaints were handled fairly and efficiently.

I found some aspects of our work and procedures gave me cause for concern. I have earlier referred to the problem of informational overkill. As I have explained, the organisation generated phenomenal amounts of paper. Governors received media extracts by the sack-full, and a huge amount of reading matter and data for information. It was a dilemma familiar to any minister in government. He or she must have a right to see everything which might conceivably be relevant; but could reading it all leave any time to actually run the department? Here a good Private Office (run by such as my college contemporary John Delafons) would be a great help in terms of filtering out, summarising, or separating the real matters needing attention from those deserving at best a quick scan.

Governors did not have Private Offices, although the three National Governors were more fortunate than their other colleagues – with the exception of the Chairman and Vice Chairman – in at least having local offices to sit in and local staff with the means and ability to support them. If Governors were not to have their own dedicated bureaucracy, other than the heavily-loaded Secretary and his or her staff, they needed to insist on good discipline in the nature and extent of the material made available to them.

Then there was, certainly for a career bureaucrat like myself, the tyranny of the agenda. Meeting even twice a month, the Board would face a crowded agenda of business. In preparation for Charter renewal, many of the issues under discussion were of real complexity and importance. Too often the Chairman would have to curtail some useful line of discussion to allow the agenda to move forward and be completed. When Christopher Bland succeeded Duke Hussey as Chairman he could on occasions show intense impatience as prolonged discussion of some contentious issue raised the risk of an uncompleted agenda. Seated around that large table, a Governor wishing to contribute to the debate would commonly raise a finger to attract the Chairman's attention. One day, I remember, as the clock moved inexorably forward, Bland intervened with some acerbity and impatience. 'I can see several people with fingers up. But we have to get on, you know.' Alas, I could not resist temptation. 'Perhaps, Chairman, you would prefer one person with two fingers up?' A self-indulgent but rather enjoyable moment in my BBC career. Bland was a most businesslike and effective Chairman, but his many virtues did not include conspicuous charm or patience.

At first, after I joined the Board, the pattern of fortnightly agenda-driven meetings was maintained. Eventually, though, a new pattern was adopted. Under this we would have monthly meetings with a more rigorously disciplined agenda, interleaved with less formal meetings without a multi-item agenda, normally held over dinner, and used to allow discussion of particularly weighty issues of current importance, often in face-to-face dialogue with the member of the Board of Management most directly responsible.

A crucial issue was, of course, the involvement of Governors in relation to programmes. Fascinating though discussions about structure, finance or personnel might be, all this elaborate and complex infrastructure existed solely to support the production of excellent programmes. It was clear to me that the main factor in maintaining the reputation of the BBC would be its ability not merely to aspire to excellence but to achieve and demonstrate it in its various genres. Why have a public service broadcaster at all, if all it did was to produce programmes of similar standards to those of its commercial rivals?

When I first joined the Board, it was a well-established practice to devote part of the time at each meeting to comments by Governors on programmes. Very occasionally we would be informed about programmes in prospect, often in the context of a wider presentation by a channel Controller or other senior manager of part of the output. I can still remember Jonathan Powell describing to us his ambitions for the new soap *Eldorado*, making the idea of 'a soap in the sun' seem a sure-fire winner. Concept and aspiration were let down by reality. The employment of inexperienced or inappropriate actors and the painfully ersatz character of the set gave, from the first screening, a painfully naff impression.

However we would never discuss programme detail, or seek to view a script or preview a programme. The *Real Lives* fiasco had been an embarrassing breach of the editorial constraints accepted in the Johnston letter, and the damage done to the Corporation by a self-evident split between Governors and management had instilled in the Board a circumspect caution about any comparable intervention. Thus our comments were essentially post facto.

I confess that initially I found our role in this area frustrating and ill-defined. In a way it could seem as absurd to detach Governors from the issue of programmes as to allow non-executive directors of a soap company to discuss anything but soap. There is, though, a dilemma here familiar to anyone who has experienced the lay involvement on professional mysteries. One could, for example, identify occasions in the world of policing where tension could arise as between a Police Authority's duty to represent the public interest and a Chief Constable's attachment to his operational autonomy.

Most members of the Board would arrive with no previous experience of programme-making, and it is not always easy to make the transition from hands-on responsibility to oversight. I doubt if his period as a Governor was Hugh Carleton Greene's most enjoyable experience at the BBC. Essentially we would be twelve individuals with personal interests and prejudices not necessarily identical with those of many members of a diverse audience. In any case the use of the singular word 'audience' can of itself be highly misleading. I often recall a television interview years ago with the press mogul and megalomaniac Cecil King. When the interviewer asked him, in effect, how a man of his evidently cultivated tastes could possibly take pride in the *Daily Mirror*, King replied; 'But I don't produce the *Daily Mirror* for people like me.' And it is, incidentally, unwise to assume that a taste different from one's own is a 'lower' taste, as if there were a table of tastes as fixed as the table of elements.

My conclusion was not that the Governors should abandon any role in relation to programmes as trustees for the public interest. They needed to understand the principal considerations underlying a particular genre of the output, so as to inform the Board before adoption, rolling forward or modification of a coherent programme strategy. The aim should not be to enable an individual Governor to say 'I liked this' or 'I didn't like that' but rather to consider whether the programmes transmitted, individually and taken together, had been consistent with a strategic approach to broadcasting having at its heart and core the public interest.

Did this mean, then, that Governors should be reluctant to comment post facto on individual programmes, and that in no circumstances whatever should they ever seek to view or hear a programme before transmission? I would not myself have wanted to carry the argument that far. It already was a well-established and generally useful practice within the BBC to submit both radio and television programmes to post facto peer review. Indeed, as I have explained, some of my earliest experiences as a Governor had involved sitting in on just such reviews. But it had to be remembered that programmes are not produced primarily to win the approbation of other broadcasters, gratifying though that will be to any producer. I reasoned that if I myself were to be responsible for the output, I would be undismayed to learn that in a general way one or two Governors had not greatly enjoyed or even approved of a particular programme. The musical policy of Radio 1, for example, was unlikely to be geared to titillate the taste of a sexagenarian retired bureaucrat. But if, on the other hand, virtually a whole Board – a group of people more heterogeneous in its tastes than was sometimes supposed – were to take the view that a particular programme or programmes had been wholly at odds with publicly-proclaimed BBC aims and standards, I hope I would want to think seriously about that reaction, without regarding constructive criticism as a direction by inference.

As far as the scrutiny of scripts or the pre-viewing or pre-listening to programmes is concerned, I felt there was a risk of over-concentration on past instances of a distinctly rare and exceptional kind. In my entire time at the BBC I had not, as a Governor, seen or heard, or wanted to see or hear, any programme whatever in advance of transmission. I had found it fascinating that, when the BBC's own *Panorama* programme had decided to focus on the question 'Whither the Corporation', and I myself had been interviewed for that programme, far more importance had been attached to a quite hypothetical role of 'censorship' than either past experience or current reality merited.

However, the BBC had long operated on the sensible basis of 'reference up'. In certain clearly-defined areas the makers of programmes had been specifically required to refer matters to higher management. I am sure this applied widely across the media. In America the Watergate journalists had needed to be sure of the backing of senior editorial staff. At home it was prudent to require consideration of the views of the Controller in Belfast before proceeding with a highly controversial programme touching on the affairs of Northern Ireland. Since, under the Charter, the Governors were the Corporation and not something detached from it, it would be difficult to argue that there were no hypothetical circumstances whatever in which the Governors might hear or view a programme in advance. It was, after all, to protect the public interest that the Governors were there at all. The real question was not whether such intervention would be lawful or proper, but whether it would be wise. I did not see it as a role for Governors, save in extremely unlikely hypothetical circumstances, to dive into editorial decisions uninvited. On the other hand, I did not see it as wrong in any way for senior management, at its own volition, to seek a second opinion. Once only did a management colleague choose to speak to me about some programme touching on Northern Ireland. I was not offered, nor did I seek, an opportunity to view the programme under discussion, and I made it clear that I would offer a view only on the understanding that the editorial decision must rest with management. It was quite clear throughout my time that Governors were not seeking to intervene prior to transmission, but of course reserved the right to make judgements afterwards on such issues as compliance with promulgated guidelines.

When I spoke in 1994 aspects of the BBC's future were still under debate prior to Charter renewal. I had long ago identified a marked tendency in Britain to take the continuity of deeply-rooted institutions as a given, and thereafter to confine the use of our critical faculties to the modest adaptation of bodies already existing almost as natural phenomena. Yet I had found that a comprehensive approach to prospective Charter renewal required us to take nothing for granted: not a continuing commitment to public service broadcasting; not its expression hitherto through the BBC as currently constituted; not to the institutional and funding arrangements which had hitherto sustained it; not to the role in its affairs hitherto played by a Board of Governors.

I was persuaded that what mattered was the task, the mission. The means of delivering it were secondary, and a fit topic for extensive and open-minded debate. At that stage I was not wholly persuaded that, in presenting our case to the public, we had fully succeeded in separating the primary from the secondary; in untangling the central role of a public broadcasting corporation in modern Britain from the immensely complex, daunting but necessary infrastructure required to support it. There had been at times, both in our internal debates and their exposure to the public, too much 'management-consultancy-speak'. At times our Director General had seemed to equate the views of the McKinsey consultants with the Ten Commandments. Since I myself had emerged into what I hoped would be the civilised light of the BBC from the dim corridors of Civil Service bureaucracy, I needed no persuasion about the necessity in the accountable modern world for strategies, plans, performance measures, accountability requirements and effective controls. As the recently-appointed chairman of the BBC Audit Committee I understood very well the need to be careful in the custodianship of very large sums of public money, albeit derived from licence fees rather than direct from taxation.

Yet in the end what mattered was making a convincing case for the maintenance in Britain of a strong, vigorous and independent public service broadcasting organisation, for very wide-ranging and fundamental cultural, artistic and social reasons. My use of the words 'cultural' and 'artistic' does not indicate a concentration on Himalayan elitism. I could see nothing indecent or second-rate about fun. In the days when the music hall and saucy postcards were elements of the British experience, they had neither competed with, or derogated from, Shakespeare or Turner. Above all they were native products; a part of the differentiating indigenous experience. While it would be absurd to exclude from our airwaves or screens all contributions, pleasing to the audience, from America or Australia or elsewhere, these should remain the leaven, not the paramount part of the lump.

After intense internal debate, the BBC's mission statement or bid for favourable Charter renewal had focused on four paramount roles:

- to ensure that issues of importance to the nation, irrespective of immediate popular effect, would be properly reported, debated and analysed;
- to reflect the full and diverse range of culture and entertainment

in modern British society;

- to increase the insights, understanding and knowledge of its audience across the full range of its programming; and
- to be, as the world's most trusted international source of news and information, culture and entertainment, one of the primary means of communication between Britain and other countries.

Personally I placed a special emphasis on two objectives entirely compatible with these headline statements of mission. I believed that as a bi-media operation (soon to be multi-media) with international, national and local capabilities, we had a particular part to play in what I thought of as 'articulating the nation'. Moving, as Governors did, to take part in public meetings around the country, I had formed a very strong impression that our listeners and viewers greatly valued a three-way process, enabling the region or locality to understand better not only itself but the nation and the wider world beyond, and that wider world to form a well-rounded view of region or locality as well as nation. 'Mirror and window' again. I saw the BBC as uniquely well-paced to play this role of promoting through communication mutual knowledge and understanding.

I was convinced that a desire to succeed overall in the delivery of our mission had to embrace a degree of tolerance of occasional failure or error. A creative cultural organisation wholly averse to risk would be a stagnant pool. I recalled how often, sitting at a perform-ance of a well-known and much-loved opera or ballet, I would read in my programme before the lights dimmed how, at its first perform-ance, and in some cases for years thereafter, it had been received with universal derision. I had become aware since joining the Board of the innate conservatism (with a small 'c') of much of our radio audience in particular. There was also a powerful loyalty not only to particular well-established programmes and artists, but even to the timetable for seeing or hearing them. Yet, it seemed to me, we needed a broadcasting organisation capable of daring as well as patience. I would not suggest for a moment that these characteristics were absent from the make-up of many distinguished programme-makers employed by our commer-cial rivals, some of whom had cut their teeth within the BBC in the first place. Nevertheless, the need to maximise subscription income or advertising revenues could at times be a constraint on programmatic adventure and experimentation. We were in real danger of entering an era of the cloning of the popular.

I felt it was more important to maintain a genuine public broadcasting organisation than to defend any single pre-existing feature of it. To this point we had consistently defended the licence fee, not because we thought any other source of revenue appalling in principle, but because so far no one had been able to identify any alternative secure base of core funding which would guarantee the essentials of independence and impartiality.

In the work leading up to the publication by the BBC of its document 'Extending Choice', the Board had taken account of the massive product of the several task forces addressing, amongst other key issues, important questions of governance. A critical stage had been reached at the Joint Boards Conference of 1992. Our rationale in coming together had not been to compile a series of justifications for the structure, role and purposes of the Board as hitherto constituted, but rather to consider anew the role (if any) to be performed in the future by a body of lay people within or without the structure of a public service broadcasting organisation facing unprecedented challenges, but clear about its central mission. So what were the options as we saw them at that time? They are, perhaps, best expressed as a series of questions.

1 Could or should one entrust the conduct of the most influential media organisation in the country, largely funded by viewers and listeners through a compulsory licence fee, to a Board of Management composed solely of broadcasting professionals?

2 Or would there be merit in a new-style BBC Board which, like so many other important organisations in both the public and private sectors, would combine the talents of full-time broadcasting executives with the business and financial skills of part-time non-executives?

3 As against these options, would there be merit in a different form of supervisory Board or Trust – the 'Board across the street' or even 'the Board across town' – which might relate either to the oversight of the BBC alone or to other and wider

responsibilities for the supervision of broadcasting?

4 In the absence of a move to a 'mixed Board' or a 'Board across the street', did the existing parameters of Charter and Licence, conventions and patterns of business and governance allow the Board of Governors to define a distinctive role, and play that role usefully without usurping the proper roles of the Director General and Board of Management?

Issues such as these had, of course, also been in the minds of those who would ultimately reach decisions following Charter review. In its Consultative Document of November 1992 the Government included amongst questions to be resolved:

> Should changes be made in the functions of the Governors and the BBC Board of Management? Should there be a Public Service Broadcasting Council either to regulate the BBC or to promote, finance and regulate public service broadcasting by the BBC and other services?

The Consultative Document had observed: 'There are those who believe that the Governors have been drawn too closely into the management of the BBC. On the other hand, others think that the Governors and the Board of Management could be merged, with the Governors becoming "non-executive directors". Governors must be – and be seen to be – a body competent to assure the independence, integrity and performance standards of the BBC as public corporation seeking to identify and meet programme needs of viewers and listeners.'

As was to be expected, the role of the Governors was one of the matters touched upon by the National Heritage Select Committee in its consideration of the future of the BBC, leading in particular to a suggestion that before the appointment of future Governors there should be an extensive and public process of consultation, designed to produce a Board 'more representative' than had hitherto been the case, and with provision for interview of a nominee by the Select Committee itself.

The motives for such a recommendation were wholly admirable. Yet the task of achieving a truly 'representative' Board could prove a testing one. A significant part of the BBC's audience would be young people struggling to make their way in the world. How many such people would be in a position to devote the necessary amount of time, even if management could be persuaded to throttle back the output of its paper factory?

And did we truly want to move, in making public appointments in our country, towards the American system of congressional hearings and the cultivation by aspiring people of 'friends on the Hill?'

Yet the wholly veiled system of appointment, as I myself had encountered it, could not be justified. Some process of advertisement of vacancies and independent interview and selection would be a great improvement. I was to reflect on all of this years later, when improbably recruited as a lay assessor to a group appointed by the General Synod to consider methods of choosing bishops in the Church of England!

When the BBC Board came to discuss these issues, we found it difficult to see how a major public service, commanding great resources raised by licence fee, could or should be assigned to an executive board of professional managers alone. In such a public service there had to be some permanent and credible means of representing and assuring the public interest. We were, of course, conscious of the devolution in the wider public sector of many important tasks to 'executive agencies' under the immediate charge of a management team headed by a chief executive. But such a team could not be accorded carte blanche. It would be for the responsible Secretary of State to approve a set of clear objectives and targets for such an agency, accompanied by robust measures of relevant performance. By good fortune I was able to bring to these discussions some personal knowledge, since I had experienced the introduction of executive agencies while still 'in harness' as a civil servant, and thereafter commissioned in retirement to carry out a 'top structure review' of the Department of Social Security, which was not only one of the largest public organisations in the country, but in the throes of 'agentisation' to bodies including the ill-fated Child Support Agency.

Yet one could not envisage the BBC as an 'agent' of government. If the kind of strategic objective-setting appropriate for (say) the Benefits Agency were to be imposed on the Corporation, it would be difficult to argue that an organisation which often, inevitably and rightly pressed upon the body politic was any longer demonstrably free from political pressure or implicit influence.

In the midst of our deliberations about governance, I was diverted to read in Paul Ferris's life of Huw Wheldon, *Sir Huge*, two versions of an insider's view of the Board of Governors. In a letter he actually sent to the Chairman of the day, Charles Hill (previously the 'radio doctor') in July 1969 Wheldon had argued that the Board 'must keep up the courage of the Corporation, keep it in bad times as well as good in the knowledge that what it presides over is a matter for pride and pleasure and not only for worry and anxiety'. Happily there also survived amongst Wheldon's personal papers an earlier draft of this passage, using rather more frank and forthright language: 'Oh hell. What the bloody Board has to do is to keep its nerve ... To hell with them.' One hardly dares to imagine his professional musings on the *Real Lives* fiasco.

At first blush, the idea of the 'mixed Board' had certain attractions. After all, full-time executives and part-time non-executives worked constructively together on the boards of many important organisations. Such a model would mean looking for directors with a very different profile from most past Governors. Some previous knowledge of, and involvement in, broadcasting could be an advantage, and other financial, commercial or personnel management experience could reinforce the in-house professionals.

Yet the BBC had to be regulated in the public interest as well as managed in its own interest. If a body of people were to have that deep involvement in the day to day running of the BBC envisaged for a 'mixed board', it would be extremely difficult to argue that those same people could stand off, make critical as well as supportive judgements if necessary, and avoid the danger or appearance of total 'capture' by the organisational machine.

So a corollary of any move to a 'mixed board' might have to be the detachment of the regulatory role, to be played by a 'Board across the street'. And here, frankly, most of us believed it desirable to continue to steer a middle course between excessive involvement and excessive detachment. We felt that if a body of people were to be in a position to guarantee to the public a broadcasting service of the necessary high standards of efficiency and integrity, they needed to be close enough to the management to make sound and realistic judgements of the possible.

Thus, in our discussions at that time, we came to the conclusion that the right model for the future relationship between the Board of Governors and the Board of Management would reserve to the Governors constitutional responsibility and ultimate accountability, and allow them to remain in sufficiently close touch with management to have an informed understanding of significant issues. It should remain their task to define the broad role and mission of the Corporation and approve the strategic plans to fulfil it, with the help of performance measures to inform their judgement. But we wished to draw a line between *governing* the BBC, as ultimate trustees for the public interest, and *managing* it.

Thus it was that we came at last to the conclusions set out in 1993 in the published document 'An Accountable BBC'. The subsequent government White Paper, 'The Future of the BBC', published in July 1994, vindicated our approach at that time. Noting that the Governors were the trustees of the national, or public, interest in broadcasting by the BBC, it affirmed that their role should be 'to look after the public's interest in the BBC, not to manage it ... to ensure that the BBC's programmes, services and other activities reflect the needs and interests of the public'. The Governors would have the responsibility for approving objectives, assessing performance, keeping in touch with audiences and making sure that complaints were properly handled. They must have a key responsibility for financial oversight and a specified role in senior staff appointments.

If one had asked the question 'Should the BBC be accountable, indeed more accountable than hitherto?', the answer would almost certainly have been affirmative. Public service and a requirement for accountability inevitably marched closely together. But accountable to whom, and in what way precisely?

These were complex and fundamental questions. Since we lived in a democracy, our elected Parliament would expect to play a significant part. It was, after all, to Government and Parliament that the BBC had to look for renewal of its Charter, for the pattern of regulation of broadcasting, for decisions about the level of the licence fee, for approval of borrowing limits and so on. Nevertheless, my own view was that the political system of the country would do well to lead its public service broadcasting organisation on a light rein. We would not be doing our duty, as an independent, impartial and reliable source of news and coverage of current affairs, if we did not from time to time ruffle and irritate politicians from all parties. They in turn must have the right, as did all our people, to criticise individual editorial or programme decisions if they thought them wrong or unfair; but they would do well to understand and if necessary defend our right to make them.

For us as Governors there would continue to be no greater responsibility than to defend robustly, and against all comers, the independence of the BBC. Most emphatically this did not mean signing up to the absurd adage 'The BBC right or wrong'. The Corporation most damaged itself when it failed to recognise the vital distinction between the right to make decisions and the ability always to make the right ones. A certain humility could be more disarming of criticism than an attitude of touchy defensiveness when criticised. I sometimes recalled how, years before, as a junior Home Office minister, George Thomas (later Speaker) had found himself at the despatch box for the first time answering questions about Northern Ireland. In all innocence he used the term 'the colony'. Cries of outrage from the Unionist benches were rapidly put to rest by the disarming admission: 'My, my. I wish I hadn't said that.' One of my heroes, Willie Whitelaw, had a similar gift for disclaiming infallibility.

Defence of the BBC did not mean or need an attitude of 'the Corporation right or wrong', but the will and capability to resist any form of pressure, direct or indirect, political or commercial, national or international. We wanted to reach the eyes and ears of people around the world, but not to be in anyone's pocket. From time to time our wholly legitimate activities would irritate or even infuriate individuals, institutions, foreign governments or states. When the BBC did so in the course of its duty and mission, the Governors had to stand absolutely firm.

None of this meant a failure to recognise the constant need to be accountable to our viewers and listeners, to those who paid the licence fee which remained our main source of income. My strong view about this aspect of accountability was that we must seek to be, in every sense and by a variety of means, accessible to listeners and viewers and respectful of their concerns; but it also had to be appreciated that a great cultural, artistic and news organisation could not determine its schedules or programme content by referendum. Indeed all talk of 'the audience' could be something of a misnomer, because the BBC of all broadcasting organisations had to recognise a special duty to that complex of minorities which makes up the whole in a diverse society.

Above all, though, that pattern of accountability which was at the heart of the Governors' role was encapsulated in the word 'trusteeship'. We had to regard ourselves as custodians for the time being of a great national treasure; a huge privilege and responsibility. We had therefore set out as clearly as we could how that responsibility should be recognised. Our ultimate authority would in particular require control of the appointment of a Director General and key senior executives; operation of a remuneration policy; and establishment of an Audit Committee on the lines envisaged by the Cadbury Report on Corporate Governance.

We accepted, on the other hand, that in most matters – including the conduct of the BBC's day to day affairs – authority would be exercised by managers on our behalf, reserving to us as trustees the role of oversight. Here, as we saw it, our responsibilities would be to stay closely in touch with public opinion; to ensure that the BBC's overall strategy reflected the needs and interests of the public; to monitor and review performance against agreed objectives; to ensure compliance with statutory requirements and BBC guidelines; and to ensure regular reporting to the licence-payer and to Parliament.

Inevitably, as one of the three National Governors, I placed real emphasis on the need for sensitivity to regional interests and concerns in our task of 'articulating the nation'. We had to reconcile the concept of 'one BBC' (later to come under severe pressure in Scotland), which was in my view part of our strength, with an awareness of, and sensitivity to, the distinct needs, traditions and aspirations of discrete parts of our United Kingdom. It was for that very purpose that Scotland, Wales and Northern Ireland had been endowed by Charter with National Broadcasting Councils concerned with the programme output specific to these 'countries'. The BBC did not have subsidiary companies or a federal system analogous with the structure at the time of independent television; nevertheless the Councils had, within their regions, some of the characteristics of the Board at the centre of the BBC. We had moved to sharpen up the functions of these Councils by providing for them a standard role in reviewing broadcasting plans and programme performance, seeking to stiffen their contacts with the communities they served, and (as an outcome of the work which I had led) providing for each of them an opportunity for direct dialogue with the Board prior to its own annual review.

Such, then, was my thinking in mid-term as a Governor. We shall see later to what extent, and why, events were to move in a direction which I did not favour then and do not favour now. But I would not wish to resile from a single word of my conclusion at Peter Hennessy's seminar when I said: 'To a child of the Thirties, such as I was, the voice of the BBC was in one's ear almost as insistently as mother or teacher. In matters of the mind and spirit the BBC was, indeed, in a very real sense, mother and teacher to many of us. I have been glad to have the opportunity to pay back some small part of the debt I owe it.'

7

THE IMPACT OF BIRT

B y now everyone knows the tale of the taxi-driver invited to a
hotel in the days when George Best was enjoying a hedonistic
lifestyle. He gazed upon the abundant champagne and the ample
form of a couple of Miss Worlds before inquiring 'Where did it all go
wrong, George?' Where did some, if not by any means all of it, go
wrong in the case of John Birt?

In an earlier chapter I have described Birt's inexorable rise to the
Director Generalship, his new vision of 'Producer Choice', and his
recovery from the 'Armanigate' embarrassment, culminating in the
recruitment of its Chief Executive to the staff of the BBC.

I now turn to the subsequent performance and record of this
controversial and ultimately divisive figure, and not least to his relationships with Duke Hussey as Chairman and to colleagues in senior
management. It is important to emphasise at the outset that, to begin
with, Birt's succession was due in no small measure to Hussey's
judgement that he would be the right man to lead the Corporation. He
had, indeed, wished Birt to succeed Checkland at once rather than after
a compromise extension of Checkland's term. It was also the case that
Birt's blind spots did not include a lack of awareness of all his own
deficiencies and vulnerabilities. He was a great protagonist of bringing
really able people with skills he admitted to be complementary with
his own, such as Bob Phillis and Liz Forgan, into the Corporation's
senior management. Yet his relationships with a number of his original
allies and admirers ended in tears. The reasons for such breaches were
complex, and differed from case to case. Private and shy man though

he was, Birt had demonstrated throughout his career an extraordinary capacity for making and retaining useful friendships with a wide range of able and influential people outside the BBC; with Blair and Mandelson, Robin Butler and Terry Burns. None of these were people to take fools gladly, and Birt was very far from being a fool.

Let us begin, then, by outlining the principal organisational, programming and other developments associated with the Birt years. In late 1992 he inherited an organisation producing some flops (such as *Eldorado*) alongside popular and critical successes (like *Absolutely Fabulous* or *Elizabeth R*). I have earlier argued that a creative organisation unwilling to take artistic risks would atrophy; but the sad case of *Eldorado* showed the danger of investing very substantial resources in projects which were challenging in principle but shoddy in practice.

In the following year Birt got into his stride. Producer Choice was unveiled, 'Armanigate' endured and survived, and the new DG began to assemble his chosen top management team. The hard-nosed Rod Lynch was recruited from British Airways to lead a new Resources Directorate responsible for all BBC facilities, Rodney Baker-Bates arrived from the Midland Bank to get a firm grip on Finance, and Pamela Taylor arrived from the BMA to handle (briefly) Corporate Affairs. However, much the most significant import was a new Deputy Director General in Bob Phillis. In discussion with the Governors, Birt had recognised the need to draw on some skills complementary with his own, and he had made it clear that he believed Bob, hitherto Chief Executive at ITN, to be just that man. His primary tasks would be to manage the BBC World Service, oversee the new facilities division and develop the commercial activities of the BBC.

Here I digress briefly to reflect on the extraordinary diversity of activity confronting a new Governor such as myself, willing and indeed anxious to see at first hand all these activities. I made fascinating sorties to Bush House, home of the World Service, where I could listen to staff speaking to the world in numerous different languages. That service remained radio-borne and was indeed beamed to some parts of the world where television ownership was a rarity. These programmes were funded by the Foreign and Commonwealth Office, whereas when BBC World television came along it had to look to other sources of funding. The World Service was rightly seen, but not always sufficiently valued, as an important arm of the UK's external relations, and gained respect as being a purveyor of truth rather than propaganda. Its credibility crucially depended on its demonstrable independence even from the government which funded it; on its determination to tell the truth as objectively as it could, so that many people in distant lands would prefer its version of events in their own country to the crudely slanted or heavily censored version emanating from the local state, or state-dominated, broadcaster. There were, as we shall see later, sometimes penalties to be paid for this independence and resistance to commercial or political pressure. In too many countries, regimes looked upon truth as a dangerous virus.

I also made a point of visiting the BBC monitoring establishment at Caversham. It was a venue out of science fiction; an old-fashioned country house festooned with, and surrounded by, impressive discs tilted to receive remote radio and television signals. In no sense was it part of an 'intelligence' operation. It did not 'intercept' but received programmes openly broadcast from Russia and other places. Some of the information so gleaned had commercial value when summarised and made available. For example, those interested in gambling in commodity 'futures' would take a keen interest in detailed reports of climatic conditions in remote places. Political upheaval could sometimes be inferred or suspected as a result of an unexplained failure to transmit expected programmes. The earliest indication of turmoil in the Soviet Union, centred around the coup against Gorbachev, was a sudden and unannounced decision to depart from normal programme sequences on Soviet radio. As in so many areas, Britain shared its insights with the USA. Under the aegis of the CIA Americans watched or listened to programmes not covered by BBC monitoring, and made the product available to the UK on a reciprocal basis. I repeat, such monitoring was distinct from intelligence activity, from SIGINT derived through communications surveillance or HUMINT derived from agent sources.

Of course as a senior official I had a degree of knowledge of these more covert activities. No doubt this is why, when I planned a holiday in China, a gentleman from a shadowy agency came to warn me of the possibility of entrapment or compromise. In the event, an approach was made to me on my very first day in Peking (as we still called it). Our guide from the official Chinese tourist service was a Mrs Fen, pronounced rather ambiguously as 'Mrs Fun'. Her English was accurate if strongly accented. As we passed block after block of faceless apartments, Mrs 'Fun' would appear to say 'Here are flats of garment workers' and 'Here also are flats of garment workers'. Only when I probed her about the apparent extent of the local trade in garments and textiles did I realise that she had been referring to 'government workers'.

At all events, as we made our way back to our Peking hotel, Mrs 'Fun' approached me in confidential fashion. 'You seem to be educated person. Perhaps we can have quiet word when we get back to hotel.' 'Oh, ho,' I thought, 'the honey-trap is being set very early.' I did not know whether to be disappointed or relieved (Mrs. Fen being a middle-aged lady of no particular allure) when she sat me down in the busy hotel lobby, produced a notebook and pencil, and asked, 'I am not sure I am understanding all the English history from the primitive times. Perhaps you would explain to me?' So I found myself conducting an improbable seminar, jogging forward from Magna Carta through the Bill of Rights to universal suffrage. Neither Bush House nor Caversham would afford me such an experience. Perhaps, I reflected, Burgess had been drawn to the Soviet Union by a mutual interest in Baudelaire or the career of William Ewart Gladstone.

Another early BBC sortie took me to the offices of the *Radio Times*, at the time the most popular magazine in Britain. Later I would attend a reception for people who had appeared on its familiar cover. Shortly before my visit to the offices, BBC Northern Ireland, for reasons unknown to me, had arranged for me to be photographed with Elizabeth. As I made my way around, the editor asked 'Would you like to see next week's cover?', at which point Lynford Christie of Olympic fame appeared on a desk-top screen. Then, 'You may like to see another cover', and there emerged this picture of Liz and myself in the form of a spoof *Radio Times* cover, accompanied by captions like 'Good sports. Meet the athletic Bloomfields ... he's in the swim and she's queen of the court' and 'DIY. We did up Stormont Castle'. We still have a framed copy of this plausibly authentic cover, and visitors to our home are greatly impressed by apparent evidence that we featured all those years ago on the cover of the *Radio Times*. The reference to tennis was very apt. Liz has played it with passion and some skill from childhood to the present day, and we have been fortunate enough to be spectators at Wimbledon on many occasions.

To return, though, to John Birt's 'imports'. Bob Phillis was, in social terms, the polar opposite of our rather impenetrable DG. Coming to us from an impressive career in newspapers and independent television, he seemed well suited to be a most useful foil to John; cheerful, amiable, communicative and efficient.

Birt had also persuaded Liz Forgan to throw in her lot with the BBC. A noted writer and broadcaster, she joined us from a very senior position at Channel 4 to become Managing Director of Network Radio, replacing in that role the delightful David Hatch. Liz was full of energy, buzzing with ideas and enormously articulate and convincing. Accompanying her later to the lobby group 'The Voice of the Viewer and Listener', I witnessed a stunning defence of the BBC and its standards.

The arrival of Phillis and Forgan in particular could be compared with the coup of a new Premier League manager bringing into the club two star players of high reputation and proven ability. Yet neither would 'stick' in the BBC in the long term. The reasons for their leaving (Forgan in 1996 and Phillis in 1997) were, as I shall explain, different and complex. Had their 'form', to pursue the footballing analogy (and Birt was much attached to football), not been up to expectations, or did they not fit comfortably into the strategy pursued by the DG? In a moment we will look at the development of that strategy and its repercussions.

While Forgan's recruitment represented an importation of undeniable talent, it was at the cost of a rather brutal sidelining of the late David Hatch. In his later (and not wholly reliable) memoir, *The Harder Path*, Birt would describe David as 'close to retirement'. He was in fact, at the relevant time, 54 years old, which is hardly in these days the 'sere and yellow leaf'. A classic BBC man through and through, he had been with the Corporation, in positions of increasing responsibility, since

1964. Cheerful, funny, inventive, loyal and universally liked, he could justify Will Wyatt's description of the BBC as 'the fun factory'. In an increasingly earnest world of McKinsey consultants and diagrammatic solutions, Hatch embodied the principle of enjoyment. Loyal servant of the Corporation that he was, he accepted, and occupied until 1995, an ambiguous role of Adviser to the Director General. I am sure he offered Birt much good advice; less sure how much impact it had on Birt's policies and approach.

Both the sidelined Hatch and the short-term imports would go on to great things after quitting the BBC; Sir David Hatch as chairman of the Parole Board, Liz Forgan as Chair of the National Heritage Memorial Fund and Sir Robert Phillis as Chairman of the Guardian Media Group.

We were entering a period of great change. From its radio beginnings with Reith, the BBC had developed into a colossal organisation owning its own production and transmission systems and the infrastructure to support them. The retirement of Thatcher had removed a Prime Minister wholly antipathetic to the BBC, but it continued to face regular accusations of being over-powerful, over-ambitious, anti-competitive, politically biased and wasteful in its use of resources. There were strong external pressures to 'cut the BBC down to size'. That process had begun with a statutory imposition in 1990 that the BBC must buy in 25 per cent of its programmes from the independent sector, and this of itself stimulated a rapid growth in that sector. We were to become well used to seeing, above the concluding logo 'BBC MCMLXXV' the rubric 'Produced by Dracula Productions' or 'Dorian Gray Enterprises' or whatever.

Then, in 1993, through Producer Choice, Birt had created, for better or worse, an internal market within the BBC. Under pressure from regions outside London, and following up a landmark report by David Hatch, the Corporation introduced a principle of 'regional proportionality', under which 33 per cent of all network television output would come from the BBC centres in Bristol, Birmingham and Manchester, together with Scotland, Wales and Northern Ireland. A centre such as Bristol, with its dedicated unit for Natural History programmes, entered this new era with an inbuilt advantage. It should, however, be emphasised that the outworking of the new principle did not assure any of these several production centres of an assured or allocated quota of its own. Those in a position to commission programmes would consider what, in effect, were competing 'bids' from the different centres around the country. A great deal of the time of regional managements would be spent lobbying in London. While aiming at the overall outcome, the BBC would rightly not commission sub-standard offerings. Of course the commissioners were, in the nature of things, judging well-defined and well-argued projects rather than completed programmes. No production centre could possibly produce a programme 'on spec', only to find it rejected by commissioners as falling below the quality threshold. Advocacy and established reputation would be great assets in this process. In my own region, for instance, we were lucky enough to have a drama producer of high reputation, who helped us to build up a network presence from a very low base. However a drama or series commissioned through BBC Northern Ireland might be made by an independent and not necessarily shot wholly, or even in part, in Northern Ireland.

On her arrival at the BBC, Forgan with Alan Yentob launched a fundamental review of programme strategy, looking in particular for evidence of failure to reach adequately important sectors of the potential audience. Matthew Bannister, as a new Controller of Radio 1, controversially dispensed with some of the station's older hands and over time began to recover elements of a younger audience who had been drifting to commercial radio. An abortive and unpopular effort to dedicate Radio 4's long-wave frequency to continuous news was abandoned for the better course of establishing a new Radio 5 Live dedicated to news and sport.

The pace and direction of change at the BBC began to produce reactions of discomfort or outright opposition. We had Mark Tully, the Delhi correspondent and something of a BBC icon, criticising Birt for a failure to understand the values of the Corporation. We had Dennis Potter using a platform at the Edinburgh Television Festival to launch an extraordinarily bitter attack on both Birt and Hussey, who were described as 'a couple of croak-voiced Daleks' who could not 'appear benevolent even if you dress one of them in an Armani suit and call the other Marmaduke'. It is worth noting, too, that on the retirement from the Board of Joel Barnett he was replaced as Vice Chairman by Lord (Michael) Cocks, a former Labour Chief Whip in government, but deeply sceptical of such modern phenomena as management consultants, structural reorganisation, or other pursuits of what he termed 'the chattering classes'. At first I could make nothing of him. Frequently at Board meetings he would say nothing at all. At our more private dinners he would sometimes gaze morosely out of the window muttering, not quite under his breath, 'Not good. Not good.' However socialist he may have been in politics, he was far from being a social radical. I can still recall his stertorous sighs as a rather precious young man organised us for a group photograph of the Governors to appear in the Annual Report. He got on well with Duke Hussey, who was beginning to get cold feet about Birt's zeal in turning the Corporation upside down; this was not to be the case with Hussey's successor, Christopher Bland.

One of the main developments of 1994 underlined the BBC's determination not to trim the news coverage in transmission to foreign countries to satisfy the sensitivities of totalitarian regimes. We had become reliant, for television outreach into mainland China, on Murdoch's Star satellite. It became clear that the Chinese would impede Star reception in China if it continued to carry BBC material not universally favourable to the Chinese regime. The BBC came to the reluctant but principled conclusion that, rather than 'trim' its relevant coverage it would withdraw its availability on the Star satellite. This probably came as a great disappointment to many individual Chinese; on my sole visit there I had discovered a massive interest in all things British and a passionate determination to master our language. A certain Miss Flowers, who gave English lessons via Chinese radio, was much the best known English person in China at that time.

Right up to Charter renewal there remained a faction within government who would have been happy to reduce the BBC to the role of a mere 'publisher' of programmes made by others. As such it would no longer need its own infrastructure of facilities, but would seek through the broadcasting marketplace bids to make programmes meeting a 'public interest' test. This potential emasculation may well have been averted for a time by the arguments of 'Extending Choice'. Yet the

Birt decision, effective from 1996, to split the organisation between BBC Broadcast (to be headed by Will Wyatt) and BBC Production (to be headed by Ron Neil) represented a move in this direction, in that Broadcast could, did and (in terms of the 'independents' quota') had to look outside as well as inside the Corporation for its commissioned programmes, whereas Production seemed fated to represent a diminishing ghetto. We were moving along a road on which the transmission system, most of the support facilities and services and even (for a time) control of its own property portfolio would drift away from the BBC. This is the setting in which to consider further the interaction between Birt on the one hand and Hussey, Phillis and Forgan on the other.

John Birt is on record as believing that his alienation from Hussey began with the plaudits rained upon him for 'saving the BBC', when the Major Government's White Paper made it clear that the Charter would be renewed on broadly acceptable terms. I am not a mind-reader, and cannot know whether there was any substance in this, although I find it difficult to believe that the Hussey I knew could be so small-minded. What was becomingly increasingly clear was that the Chairman had become apprehensive about the rate of change and its impact on morale within the organisation. Even when surgery is necessary to keep a patient alive, nobody enjoys losing a limb. Reorganisation involved substantial redundancies and a growing uncertainty about the future. Some at least of the 'creative people' had found Checkland (from an accountancy background) more sensitive to creative processes and people than Birt (from a programme-making background).

By the 1995 Board conference relations between the two men had sunk to a low level. At one point Hussey, to the DG's great resentment, had excluded management from a session where he had expressed a growing concern. An already bad relationship worsened as Birt brought forward a radical plan to bring together in a single News Centre all those concerned with news and current affairs, whether on radio or television. The decision of the Governors to back Birt on this issue had serious repercussions. Liz Forgan had considered the proposed fusion wrong-headed and had argued strongly against it. Hussey himself had growing reservations. Birt won the day, but at the heavy cost of losing Forgan and further alienating Duke Hussey.

In retrospect I regret not having identified myself with the Forgan case. Not only was it tragic to lose her, after she had shown such talent, but it is not always wise, in the interests of 'tidiness', to override old loyalties and traditions. BBC Radio transmitted from Broadcasting House represented the very roots of the BBC. Amalgamation of distinguished regiments has been part of the army experience, but sometimes much has been lost in terms of prestige, morale and appeal. Radio and television journalism are very different disciplines. There are, of course, some authentic bi-media people, but many famous broadcasters are much better suited to one mode than the other. Wogan, so affably at home on radio, as if chatting from his own fireside or from the snug of a pub in his native Ireland, always seemed to me stiff, uncomfortable and contrived on television. As a fairly regular contributor to both media, I had become philosophical about those long interviews on film, usually reduced on screen to a minute or two at most, and sometimes focusing on the least relevant of the points one had sought to make. By comparison, radio could still offer civilised and intelligent dialogue. Of course consolidation is commonly justified by a search for 'savings', but the capital of an organisation in the cultural sphere does not rest solely on a head-count. Having fought hard and lost on an issue about which she felt strongly, Liz decided, as a matter of principle, to leave the BBC. She was much missed by all of us; not least by myself in spite of earning chastisement when driving her around Belfast in my own car, when she found I was tuned in to Classic FM.

The relationship between Birt and Bob Phillis also deteriorated. The DG seemed to feel that Phillis was not pushing hard enough to develop and exploit commercial opportunities. For his part Bob understandably resented an unwillingness to consult him about radical changes introduced as a virtual fait accompli. He felt he had a right to be treated with more respect. So in 1997 Phillis also decided to leave the BBC. I thought him a great loss; a man of integrity and common sense with a human touch absent from the Birt personality. Birt had introduced Phillis to us as a person with skills complementary with his own. He was right about that, but failed in the event to take full advantage of those skills.

The last straw, in terms of holding Chairman and Director General together in a decent and constructive relationship, was the remarkable episode of the Martin Bashir interview with Diana, Princess of Wales. By this time the tale of the alienated princess had become a soap opera comparable with the more imaginative episodes of *Dallas*. That beautiful but rather disturbed young woman had believed herself to be a victim of character assassination as well as of her husband's relationship with Camilla Parker-Bowles, and Bashir, in a brilliant journalistic coup, had persuaded her to grant him a long interview for *Panorama* in which she would present her side of this sad and deeply regrettable story. With the BBC protocols concerned with 'reference up', there was no way in which Bashir could hide his project from senior management. Bashir very properly briefed Tony Hall, the Director of News and Current Affairs, and Hall in turn told Birt.

It was inconceivable that anyone in BBC management, at any level, would have wished to impede transmission of this interview. Diana was fully entitled to express her views and feelings; these would be of huge interest to millions of people in the UK and around the world, and any broadcasting organisation worth its salt would have sat up and begged for such an opportunity.

There was, though, one complicating factor. Since Governors had learned their lesson from the *Real Lives* fiasco, there was virtually no prospect of the Board seeking to impede or interfere in any way with the programme. Yet one could see any Chairman, unexpectedly viewing on his television the most sensational programme of his term, asking himself if he should not at least have been given fair warning of the impending *coup de théâtre*. There was, though, a substantial complication. By 1995 Duke Hussey's wife, Lady Susan Hussey DCVO, had been a lady-in-waiting to the Queen for some thirty-five years, and had become over time not just a courtier but a real personal friend to Queen Elizabeth and other members of the Royal Family. On numerous royal visits at home and abroad Lady Susan had been the monarch's closest and most intimate companion. To tell Hussey about the programme well in advance would put him in a most embarrassing and invidious position. In the light of the *Real Lives* experience any effort to preview an interview, by himself alone or alongside other Governors, could prove very damaging to all within the BBC. Members of the royal family, on the other hand, might have found it hard to understand why, knowing about it, he had done nothing to prevent it.

I would not myself, in these unique circumstances, be critical of Birt's response to the situation, save for feeling that he might at least have put the Vice Chairman, Michael Cocks, in the picture. While Governors were right to be very slow about intervening in editorial matters, this did not mean that broadcasters themselves should consider themselves barred from taking advantage of the judgement and experience of people who understood the mores of the Corporation and could offer a view, to be accepted or rejected, in compete confidence. I could recall from my days as a student historian the implications of the famous 'Campbell case' in the 1920s, involving the role of the Attorney General as prosecuting authority. The proposition had been asserted that, while the Cabinet could not instruct the Attorney to prosecute or not, he himself was entitled to take soundings there or anywhere else before reaching an independent judgement as to whether prosecution would be in the public interest. It is not, I think, a totally absurd analogy, because after all the prime task of Governors was to protect the public interest.

Inevitably, though, the controversial episode did nothing to heal the growing and damaging breach between Birt and Hussey. The Chairman who had initially been so avid for the Birt succession had become increasingly disenchanted with the environment of incessant change and 'rationalisation', the extensive and mounting costs of hiring management consultancy gurus, and the atmosphere of Stalinist dogmatism which had come to dominate the organisation. It had been a triumph of courage and willpower for Hussey to rise above his appalling wartime injuries, to accept no constraint upon his activities despite endless pain and discomfort, and to throw himself heart and soul into the governance of a great national institution.

I had seen, since 1991, many sides of his character. Occasional bursts of petulance and temper, yes; but on the whole, with trusted colleagues, affability and good humour. Normally he got his own way, but as much by charm and persuasion as anything else. Often parodied as a quintessential establishment figure, he would encounter junior BBC staff at provincial centres with genuine warmth. He believed that human life existed outside the rigid circle of serious endeavour; he was Cavalier rather than Roundhead. At the end of a long and hospitable evening in his suite at some BBC event outside London, one would retire to bed with a sense of enjoyment (if sometimes with a throbbing headache). I am not sure that he had a great cultural hinterland. On one occasion when the Queen came to a Prom at the Royal Albert Hall, it was easy to observe from the next box that that she would rather have been at Royal Goodwood than at the Royal Albert Hall. Meeting Lady Susan at the interval, I expressed surprise that the monarch had not been at a Prom before. Rather disarmingly she replied: 'If they hadn't made Dukey Chairman of the BBC, I don't suppose he would have been at one either.' On a later occasion the Queen visited Broadcasting House, and it had been my pleasure, as by then a very senior Governor, to introduce colleagues to her.

At all events, Dukey had now had enough of the BBC and John Birt. Towards the end of 1995 it was clear that we would soon be having a new Chairman. I learned of the successor in odd circumstances. For some time my daughter Caroline had been employed in the Philippines by a French NGO, Quart Monde ('Fourth World') to provide street libraries and other services for deprived children in the capital, Manila. I had decided to visit her, leaving Heathrow on Boxing Day to travel to Manila via Dubai. My airline of choice was Emirates, of whom I could not speak too highly. By then long-haul aircraft were equipped with visual displays informing passengers of precise location, expected arrival time, outside temperature and other parameters. In the case of Emirates this included an indication of the direction to, and distance from, Mecca. I recalled my visit years before to a mosque in China. 'Here,' had said the imam, 'is where we pray, facing West towards Mecca.'

It proved to be a fascinating if exhausting trip. As I lay on my first night under a single sheet yet sweating from every pore, Caroline commented that it was one of the coolest nights since she had arrived in Manila. We strolled through Rizal Park, were entertained with incredible lavishness in Forbes Park, the Belgravia of Manila, travelled up a mountain to the age-old rice terraces of Banaue in northern Luzon and spent an idyllic few days on a coral islet off the coast of Mindoro.

On return, we once again broke our journey in Dubai, where I took the opportunity to buy some English newspapers. So it was there that I read that Hussey's successor would be Sir Christopher Bland. I was to find that chance had endowed Bland with a most misleading surname; rather as if Twiggy's real name had been Miss Gross. I recalled briefly meeting him some years before at one of the annual encounters of a do-gooding body called the British-Irish Association. Organised in those days by Marigold Johnson, the wife of the choleric Paul who had made a spectacular shift from the extreme Left to the far Right, this organisation would bring together in an Oxbridge college a gathering sometimes described as 'toffs against terrorism'. One would, indeed, encounter there the odd Astor or Guinness (in the latter case both in the personal and the liquid form), but few if any representatives of the main active players in the endless and agonising Northern Ireland conflict. The conference always provided an enjoyable weekend, from which one retired with some fascinating aperçus. One regular attender would be the artistic and feyly beautiful Lindy Guinness, Marchioness of Dufferin and Ava and chatelaine of the great house, Clandeboye, close to our home. 'Do you by any chance know Andy Warhol?' she had asked me one evening. 'No, although of course I know who he is.' 'I really love him. He's like a walking corpse.' In any league of non sequiturs this remark would come very high.

Christopher Bland's interest arose out of strong connections with Northern Ireland. The son of an itinerant executive in the oil business, he had spent part of his early education in Northern Ireland at Mourne Grange School in County Down, and had qualified to fence for Ireland in the 1960 Olympic Games. Clearly nature had equipped him for the cut and thrust; the battle with unbated weapons. His charming wife Jennifer was a daughter of an Ulster politician well known to me from my early days as a civil servant in Belfast. Morris May had been a tall, authoritative, good-looking and self-confident man who – if he had lived – would have been a serious contender to succeed the ageing and lethargic Viscount Brookeborough as Prime Minister of Northern Ireland. Unhappily the curse of cancer intervened; May's life was tragically cut short; in the end Terence O'Neill inherited the poisoned chalice, and the rest is history.

The important thing to remember about Bland, as he arrived to fill the Chairman's seat, was that – unlike his predecessors – he came to the job with prior knowledge and experience of broadcasting and an extensive range of contacts made over the years with important people in that industry, as well as in politics and public affairs. A former Chairman of the Conservative Bow Group, he had joined the Board of London Weekend Television, having already served from 1972 as Chairman of the Independent Broadcasting Authority. In 1984 he had succeeded John Freeman as Chairman at LWT, and had worked closely there with John Birt and Greg Dyke. Bland and Dyke would be substantial beneficiaries of the eventual buy-out and takeover of LWT, a bonanza which Birt missed because he had moved to the BBC.

I first met Bland in his new role, before he had formally taken over, when he summoned me to see him at his office as Chairman of the National Freight Corporation, one of the many commanding positions he was to occupy in public and commercial life. On first impressions he was brisk, businesslike, well-informed but without warmth.

Overall he was to prove 'a good thing' for the BBC; at times like a dose of therapeutic if not particularly palatable medicine. From the beginning he understood, as Birt did, the challenges and opportunities represented by new and emerging technologies and the growing diversification in the broadcasting marketplace. One of my striking recollections from my final years as a Governor is of the occasional presentations to our Board by our in-house 'boffins' to show where technology might be taking us. In almost every case they proved right about the direction but substantially underestimated the rate of change. It all happened much more rapidly than even the well-informed thought likely. Birt would make a point of keeping in touch with leading-edge practitioners across the Atlantic, and could see earlier than most the implications of 'convergence', with a single versatile instrument capable of receiving telephone or text messages, music, photographic images, television or film. In all of this Patricia Hodgson was a most valuable and intellectually distinguished ally. Some, as I have made clear, criticised her as 'cold'; I did not, but instead admired the grasp of her intellect and the lucidity of her explanations and presentations.

Of course information technology had begun to penetrate the

civil service in my final years there. There would be talk of something called 'e-mail' and other facilities, originally seeming far removed from my own pattern of work. Yet how soon it would be before colleagues would sit before batteries of screens in open-plan offices. In the late 1990s only a few of the BBC Governors, many of us in late middle age, were 'on the net'. Realising how important it was that all Governors should grasp fully the powerful impact of developing information technology, we were all provided with home computers and if necessary given basic instruction on their use. I was close to retirement from the Board when this happened, nearing the end of my second term, and so I had the benefit of the BBC 'kit' only for a year before I had to return it. But by then I was totally hooked. Now in retirement I use e-mail every day, type slowly on the word processor as I write books, articles or speeches, and more and more use the BBC's own excellent website as my surrogate newspaper. Each day I work methodically through a hierarchy of world, national, local and sports news. I can, if I want to be more than usually narcissistic, listen to audios of interviews I have given on BBC Northern Ireland, watch television programmes in which I have appeared, or hear the speech I made at Stormont in 1998 when launching with Mo Mowlam my report on the victims of 'the Troubles'. It has enabled me to find out things about my own ancestry I never knew; that, for instance, in 1850 my great-great-grandfather George William Bloomfield, serving with the Royal Artillery in a fort on Scattery Island in the mouth of the River Shannon, married a local girl from the island, Bridget McMahon, giving me (a son of parents who arrived from England in 1929) an Irish lineage I had never expected.

Of my eight years as a Governor I had served almost five under the chairmanship of Duke Hussey and I would now spend a final three under Christopher Bland. When he arrived work on a publication to be called 'Extending Choice in the Digital Age' was well advanced, renewal of the Royal Charter for a further ten years was imminent, and we faced a period of stability in the sense that we now had a Chairman and Director General who had worked closely together in the past and had mutual confidence in each other. Although, as I shall explain, I was to find Bland on occasions brusque and domineering, it was a relief to move out of the atmosphere of growing animosity which had soured the final rather sad years of the Hussey/Birt relationship. Indeed the period from 1996 to 1999, when I left the Board, was to be one of change and excitement as the Corporation adapted to a rapidly changing technological environment.

In 1996 we had the launch of 'Expanding Choice in the Digital World' making clear the determination of the BBC to be to the fore in the exploitation of new technology, followed in 1997 by the launch of BBC America and BBC Choice on digital. The Corporation survived a brush with Parliament on plans to abolish the long-standing 'Yesterday in Parliament', provoking the wrath not only of Gerald Kaufmann, an unvarying scourge of the BBC, but of other basically well-disposed parliamentarians, and had to make prudent concessions. In 1999, my final year on the Board, we had the launch of BBC Knowledge.

Certainly Birt's final years under the chairmanship of Christopher Bland were free of the strains attendant on the collapsed Birt/Hussey relationship. He had been in his own way a remarkable figure; the description 'Birtism' like 'Thatcherism' characterises a distinctive era. In some odd ways this man of the left and woman of the right had common characteristics. Of each it could be said that they did things which badly needed to be done to assure the health of Corporation or nation, but that each went too far, stayed too long, and made too many enemies amongst those close to them. It is illuminating to compare the verdict of Will Wyatt, a senior and loyal colleague, with that of Dyke, who dismantled some aspects of the Birt revolution. Wyatt, writing after his retirement, would comment on tensions arising from people close to Birt; people who did his bidding in demanding more and more and erred on the side of excess. Annual performance reviews had been over-elaborate and objective-setting 'over the top'. While Producer Choice had driven down costs (saving more than £50 million in the first year to the benefit of programme budgets) the system at the outset had been too complicated, creating no fewer than 485 'business units' and at the outset involving one third of the transactions at a value of less than £100. The grip was somewhat relaxed over time, but the resentment remained. Wyatt's observations of the reaction to Dyke (after he himself had retired) were implicit criticisms of Birt. He made good appointments, was fun to work with, had made himself visible across the Corporation, and had improved the standing of local radio. Dyke, after his own departure, said that he had found fear and loathing of Birt on the part of many people working for the BBC. He had found it necessary to re-structure the organisation, take out several layers of management, put more programme people on the BBC Executive, cultivate more collaboration and move faster and less bureaucratically. He had sought to change the culture without resort to consultants, management jargon and imposition of change from above without consultation with those affected. For myself I found it intriguing to work with a flawed but fascinating man. If one could have merged Birt with Dyke (admittedly a grotesque encounter even in the imagination) one might have produced the ideal Director General, with the meticulous thoroughness and extraordinary endurance of the one married to the energy and flair of the other. What an irony that while the BBC wrestled with No. 10 during the Gilligan affair, one DG was at Broadcasting House and the other a special advisor to the Prime Minister.

8

THE ARRIVAL OF GREG DYKE

I have explained how I had witnessed the accelerated departure of Michael Checkland and the coronation of John Birt. Having seen one Director General already selected take office, I would now be involved in the selection of another who would succeed Birt after my departure from the Board.

Christopher Bland, who had been involved in various capacities over the years in appointments to senior positions, had a very clear view of how he wanted to proceed. There would, very properly, be open advertising for the post, allowing all-comers inside or outside the Corporation to be considered. To advise on the process and promote interest in application for the position a leading firm of head-hunters, Heidrick and Struggles, would be involved. There would be an initial selection panel to advise on the shortlisting of candidates for interview by the full Board. All of this was, on the face of it, fair and objective. There would be no mere coronation, as in the choice of Birt to succeed Checkland. I now believe, though, that although we would go through the appropriate motions, Bland had been quite determined from the outset to have Greg Dyke.

Looking back on it I should – as the most senior Governor then serving – have smelled a rat in my frankly rather insulting exclusion from the 'selection panel' chosen by Bland, on which he would be joined by the Vice Chairman Baroness Young; Roger Jones, the National Governor for Wales; Richard Eyre, the former Director of the National Theatre; and Pauline Neville-Jones a retired diplomat of great experience. These were all admirable people and far from being 'creatures' of the Chairman; but I suspect Bland had come to regard me as something of a loose cannon because on occasions I had failed to hide my resentment at his brusque and domineering ways.

It was important throughout to preserve as much confidentiality as possible about the names of potential candidates. People would assume, rightly, that these would include figures from the existing senior management of the BBC, and the name of Greg Dyke was also being canvassed at an early stage. On the other hand, we did not want to embarrass senior figures from outside who could suffer a backlash from existing employers if appearing to be footloose, or lose face if ultimately unsuccessful. For these reasons interviews would be conducted at obscure locations well away from Broadcasting House, where lurking paparazzi might well put two and two together as a well-known face entered the building. At the stage where I became involved, and I presume at the previous stage, Governors would leave Broadcasting House in a series of taxis for an undisclosed destination, usually the kind of flat in which a Middle Eastern potentate might maintain a London mistress. Greg Dyke himself, in his book *Inside Story*, chose to tell the world that the four candidates left in the field after initial screening were two of the in-house candidates, Mark Byford and Tony Hall, and two people from the Pearson Group, the American Michael Lynton and himself (then at Pearson Television).

Christopher Bland decided to ask Birt to give Governors views on the internal candidates, which seemed to me to be analytical, balanced and sensible. His analysis represented information rather than advocacy. One could be charitable and view Bland's invitation to Dennis Stevenson, chairman of Pearson plc, to give his views on the two Pearson candidates as an effort to ensure balance. I did not at all take to Stevenson, a rather domineering figure in the Bland mould, and his presentation came across to me as a piece of pure advocacy for Dyke. I note, too, a passage from Will Wyatt's charming book *The Fun Factory* recording a conversation at that time with Patricia Hodgson to the effect that 'Robin Young, the permanent secretary at DCMS, is going around telling everyone that Christopher came to see him to say that he was going to have Greg by hook or by crook'. So much for an open-minded selection procedure; though, to be fair, Hussey in his time had been as determined to have Birt replace Checkland.

It was into this atmosphere that there exploded a press campaign focusing upon Dyke's close links with the Labour Party, as demonstrated by financial support for the party and specifically for Tony Blair. *The Times*, *Telegraph*, *Independent*, *Guardian* and other newspapers posed the question whether such a close identification with a political party made an individual unsuitable for appointment as editor-in-chief of Britain's most prestigious and influential news organisation. Intervention by the press was one thing; an intervention by politicians quite another. Above all else, Governors would react adversely to any attempt to push them around. In that context a public intervention by William Hague was profoundly unhelpful to the cause he supposed he was advancing. Like others, I did not intend to be swayed in my judgement by pressure from this or any other politician; on the other hand I would not allow it to override my personal responsibility to reach my own conclusions without fear or favour. Of course senior managers at the BBC, like other people, had every right to their own political views and loyalties. John Birt himself, although he had worked well with Tory ministers, was clearly a man of the left, and had many close friends amongst Labour politicians, including Tony Blair himself. But there was something 'in your face' about Dyke's Labour loyalties, as indeed about Greg Dyke himself.

I met him at last when he came to be interviewed by the full Board. I did not take to him. I thought him cocky and self-confident, a populist, an entertainer. He was likely to make a happier and jollier BBC, to appeal more than the introverted Birt to creative staff, to build audiences through programmes responsive to the public taste. All of these would be great strengths in some of our competitors. Yet the 'mix' of the BBC brand also involved a degree of seriousness and heavyweight authority.

Personally I was impressed by the qualities of Mark Byford as an internal candidate. This solid, amiable Yorkshire figure (son of a former Chief Inspector of Constabulary and Chairman of Yorkshire County Cricket Club) had shown himself to be a very safe pair of hands in a number of increasingly important management posts. By now 41 years of age, he had been in succession Director of Regional Broadcasting and of the World Service. I felt he suffered from a widespread feeling that, after the Birtist revolution, it was 'time for a change'. I have no doubt that, if appointed, he would have made the Corporation a happier place, and revisited some of the more extreme aspects of the Birt regime. But he had been a senior and loyal member of Birt's management team, and he was too decent a man to pour scorn on a record to which he (like the interviewing Governors) had contributed. Yet I could see strong arguments at this stage in our history for the promotion of an authentic BBC figure. He would, I think, have shared my view that we were not 'just another broadcaster'.

I have to say that I find John Birt's account of these events in *The Harder Path* to be unreliable and unconvincing. His account gives the impression that he was more than happy to see Greg Dyke succeeding him all along. In spite of their previous association and mutual interests, I believe he felt Dyke to be unsuitable and would have preferred Mark Byford. It is an astonishing revelation that, on the eve of the crucial interview of Dyke by the Board, he agreed at Bland's suggestion to rehearse with Dyke all the arguments required to overcome reservations felt by some of us. If this is a true account – and as far as I know it has not been disputed – I think it was quite wrong of the Chairman to suggest such an approach and quite wrong of the Director General to agree to it. Yet it appears to be corroboration of Bland's reported exchange with Robin Young.

The Board then met for a tense occasion, comparable in my mind only with the exchanges about Birt's controversial pay arrangements. Bland went round the table allowing each of us to have a say. This was to be the only occasion in eight years as a Governor when I spoke from a prepared written text; and since I have kept it, I do not have to fear inaccuracy in recollection or a suggestion of post facto justification. I used, in particular, the following words:

> We need, do we not, in dealing with politically controversial issues, to be led as editor-in-chief by someone of unimpeachable impartiality? I do not suppose for one moment that Greg Dyke, if appointed, would in practice give Labour an easy ride. Indeed, the opposite might well be the case as he leaned over backwards to avoid any accusation of bias.

I was not without support in expressing my fears and reservations, but as the meeting proceeded it became clear that a substantial majority of the Board were content to approve the appointment of Dyke. As a result I faced a moral dilemma and a disagreeable choice of options. I could permit the impression to persist that the decision had been unanimous; I could refuse to be a party to such a statement or implication; or I could openly acknowledge my dissent, resign at once from the Board, and make clear my reasons for doing so.

In the event, rightly or wrongly, I decided to tolerate an impression of unanimity. All my long working life I had supported principles of collective responsibility and corporate solidarity, in the context of which one argues a point of view vigorously but accepts the ultimate decision in the event of failing to gain sufficient support. Since I was now very close to the natural end of my second term as a Governor, a resignation could too easily appear contrived and self-indulgent. Level-headed and experienced colleagues, who unlike me would have to work with Dyke as Director General, were apparently happy with the Dyke appointment. While I feared trouble ahead, I was also conscious that Board resignations at this stage would plunge the Corporation into immediate controversy.

It gives me no satisfaction whatever to record, as I shall do, that my fears and reservations at that time came to be justified; that the BBC a few years later would be plunged into an unprecedented crisis at the cost of a splendid Chairman and a charismatic if flawed Director General; and that all of this derailed a system of governance which over the years had served the Corporation and the country well. If Birt had indeed coached Dyke, his reward would be to see his metaphorical statues toppled like a media Saddam Hussein; while an embittered Dyke would make clear his essential contempt for some of the Governors who had appointed him and for the institution itself.

Throughout this unhappy and fateful episode, I had been influenced by no political consideration whatever. While the majority of my Board colleagues may well have been Conservative or Labour in their personal convictions, we in Northern Ireland were curiously distanced from national politics. But just as there is the famous adage 'Not only should justice be done, but it should be manifestly seen to be done', so

I felt that the top-hamper of the BBC should not only eschew political linkages, but should be manifestly seen to eschew them.

When Gavyn Davies (whose wife Sue Nye was 'gatekeeper' to Gordon Brown) became Chairman, and shared with his DG Dyke a close association in the public mind with the Labour Party, it was not unreasonable to expect a particularly robust display of manifest independence in the event of any effort by the Labour Government to bully, threaten or harass the BBC. As men of honour, which I am convinced they were, they would both wish and need to demonstrate that, regardless of their previous political affiliations, they would not allow the BBC to be pushed around by any party. It is now common knowledge that, well before the Gilligan/Kelly affair – which I shall discuss later – the odiously aggressive Alastair Campbell had been firing regular warning shots across the Corporation's bows. At times we would receive glimpses on 'the box' of the curious relationship between Campbell and Tony Blair. I must say I am inclined to think twice when my friendly, smiling neighbour keeps as his pet of choice a Rottweiler rather than a Labrador.

9

BOWLED GILLIGAN, STUMPED HUTTON

For the most part I have concentrated in this book upon events of which I had personal experience during eight years as a member of the Board of Governors. I am, however, anxious before I conclude to examine the state of the Corporation today and the prospects for its future, and both present and future are or will be affected by the fallout from the extraordinary events of January 2004, arguably the most damaging in the long history of the BBC, leading as they did to the departure of Gavyn Davies, the Chairman, and Greg Dyke, the Director General. In this fateful drama the person I had known longest was Lord Hutton, a retiring Law Lord and a former Lord Chief Justice of Northern Ireland, who had been appointed by the government to consider and report on the sad events centring around the suicide of Dr David Kelly. Brian Hutton and I had been amongst a small group of Ulstermen at Oxford University in the late 1940s and early 1950s, and I would encounter him regularly on 'the Liverpool boat' as a new university term was about to begin. He had made his way to Balliol from Shrewsbury School, and even as an undergraduate studying jurisprudence he had something of the High Court about him in his manner and high, fluting voice. As a High Court Judge and later Lord Chief Justice in Northern Ireland from 1979 to 1997 he had dispensed justice in the most trying of circumstances, in which judges were amongst those most at risk of terrorist attack, and indeed brothers on the Bench had been murdered by the IRA. Ulstermen are, perhaps, more detached from national politics than any of their fellow citizens in the UK, and Hutton, whose eminent career as a jurist was coming to an end, owed no favour or loyalty to any political party.

As the BBC, government and the public waited for the publication of the Hutton Report, the general expectation was that it would attach a degree of criticism or blame to both Corporation and Government. The almost total exculpation of Government, coupled with the criticism directed at the BBC, came as a bombshell to those leading the Corporation. Gavyn Davies, while convinced that the Report had been hopelessly unbalanced, decided to step down as Chairman. Greg Dyke intended to stay put, but the remaining Governors decided he ought to quit. In my view, for reasons I shall spell out later, I thought it was right for Dyke to go, but that Davies could have stayed. But was the BBC hard done by in the Hutton Report? Had Hutton, as Dyke certainly felt, gone out of his way to avoid embarrassing the Government?

The descent into the maelstrom began early on the morning of 29th May 2003. At 6.00 a.m. BBC Radio 4 carried the usual summary of the news of the day. This summary included the following: 'A senior official involved in preparing the Government's dossier on Iraqi weapons of mass destruction has told this programme that the document was re-written just before publication to make it more exciting. An assertion that some of the weapons could be activated within 45 minutes was among the claims added at a late stage. The official claimed that the intelligence services were unhappy with the changes, which he said were ordered by Downing Street.'

Shortly afterwards, in the *Today* programme, there was an exchange between John Humphreys, a very well-known BBC broadcaster, and a much less well-known Defence Correspondent, Andrew Gilligan. Gilligan referred to 'one of the senior officials in charge of drawing up the ... dossier' as believing that 'the Government probably ... knew the 45 minute figure was wrong, even before it decided to put it in'. He went on to say that 'Downing Street, our source says, ordered it a week before publication ... to be sexed up, to be made more exciting and ordered more facts ... to be discovered'.

However, there was to be a swift rebuttal from Government sources. At 7.32 a.m. a follow-up to the original story said: 'We've just had a statement from Downing Street that says it's not true, and let me quote what they said to you; "Not one word of the dossier was not entirely the work of the intelligence agencies.'" Thereafter Gilligan, in further exchanges with Humphreys, referred to a preface to the dossier written by Tony Blair and including the words 'Saddam's military planning allows for some weapons of mass destruction to be ready within 45 minutes of an order to deploy them'. 'Now,' said Gilligan, 'that claim has come back to haunt Mr Blair because if the weapons had been that readily to hand, they probably would have been found by now. But you know, it could have been an honest mistake, but what I have been told is that the Government knew the claim was questionable, even before the war, even before they wrote it in their dossier'. And yet again Gilligan quoted as his source 'a British official who was involved in the preparation of the dossier'.

I have referred to the early Downing Street rebuttal. The serious view taken of the allegations made was underlined by the later appearance in the programme of Adam Ingram, Minister of State for the Armed Forces. I knew Ingram personally, having worked with him as a Northern Ireland Office minister prior to his movement to Defence, and developed a high regard for him as a sensible, robust and honest politician. Humphreys emphasised the central allegation that the draft dossier, after reaching No. 10, had been 'sent back to be sexed up a little. I'm using not my own words, but the words of our source, as you know'. In response Ingram declared flatly: 'That isn't true.' Nevertheless Gilligan was to pursue a very similar line that same morning on Radio 5 Live.

It of course emerged later that the anonymous source upon whom Gilligan had drawn was Dr David Kelly. He had earlier been involved in assessments of biological warfare potential both in the Soviet Union in the early 1990s, and in Iraq. He was not, however, a member of any of the intelligence services, and had not been a party to the preparation of the controversial dossier. Without the authority or permission of his employers at the Ministry of Defence, and in breach of established codes of conduct, he had made contact with Gilligan on 22nd May, a week before the broadcast allegations. It has to be said, though, that he had over time spoken regularly to the press to the advantage of both the media and government. However, his conversation with

Gilligan had not been his only contact with the BBC about the dossier. More than a fortnight before, on 7th May, he had discussed the matter with Susan Watts, Science Editor of BBC *Newsnight*, and referred to the '45 minutes claim' in terms recorded by Watts in contemporary brief shorthand notes in the terms: 'mistake to put in … A Campbell seeing something in them … NB single source … but not corroborated … sounded good'. The cautionary note struck in this record acknowledges the BBC's guideline advice to be cautious about proceeding on the basis of a single uncorroborated source, while not absolutely ruling it out.

On that fateful day of 29th May other BBC journalists probed the story. Contacted by telephone in New York, Kelly expressed continuing concern about the handling of the dossier, but – as later revealed in evidence to Hutton – in distinctly more cautious and measured terms. The 'essential quality of the intelligence provided by the Intelligence Services was fundamentally reasonable'. However 'he felt that the dossier had been presented in a very black and white way. He expressed some concern about that. I think he would have been comfortable, from what he said, that it would have been more measured, in his view.' Reflecting this contact on the *10 O'Clock News* that evening, Hewitt would say: 'I have spoken to one of those consulted on the dossier. Six months work was apparently involved. But in the final week before publication, some material was taken out, some material put in. His judgement, some spin from No. 10 did come into play.'

It was not surprising that on the following day, 30th May, Susan Watts renewed contact with Dr Kelly. She told him that, looking back over her contemporary notes of their earlier conversation, she had to remind him that 'in fact you actively referred to Alastair Campbell in that conversation'. She said that Kelly had been 'more specific than the source on the *Today* programme [probably surmising that this had been Kelly himself]'. In a revealing and significant exchange, Kelly then pointed out that 'I'm not part of the intelligence community. I'm a user of intelligence … Of course I'm very familiar with a lot of it, that's why I'm asked to comment on it … but I'm not deeply embedded into that'. He accepted that 'the word-smithing is actually quite important and the intelligence community are a pretty cautious lot on the whole but once you get people putting it/presenting it for public consumption then of course they use different words. I don't think they're being wilfully dishonest. I think they just think that that's the way the public will appreciate it best.'

Gilligan, however, held to his line both inside and outside the BBC. On the *Today* programme for 31st May he asserted: 'By that day [24th September] the dossier, described as unrevealing only four weeks before, had suddenly become very revelatory indeed. A senior figure involved in compiling it told this programme two days ago that Downing Street had applied pressure to make it sexier. This quote from a British official appeared in yesterday's *Washington Post*. "There were passionate and heated debates between Downing St. officials and intelligence officials about the contents of the dossier."'

Nor did Gilligan confine his thesis to the BBC. In an article in the *Mail on Sunday* for 1st June he returned to what his 'source' (Dr Kelly) had told him. 'We had discussed the famous Blair dossier on Iraq's weapons at our previous meeting, a few months before it was published last September. "It's not really very exciting, you know", he'd told me. "So what", I asked him now, "has changed?" "Nothing changed", he said. "Until a week before it was just like I told you. It was transformed the week before publication, to make it sexier." "What do you mean? Can I take notes?" "The classic", he said, "was the statement that WMD were ready for use in 45 minutes. One source said that it took 45 minutes to launch a missile and this was misinterpreted to mean that WMD could be deployed in 45 minutes. There was no evidence that they had loaded conventional missiles with WMD or could do so anything like that quickly." I asked him how this transformation happened. The answer was a single word "Campbell." "What? Campbell made it up?" "No, it was real information. But it was included against our wishes because it wasn't reliable."'

This round of 'disclosures' emanating from Dr Kelly concluded with a further appearance by Susan Watts on *Newsnight* on 2nd June. Reflecting her exchanges with Dr Kelly on 30th May, Watts carefully repeated the words used in that encounter, to which I have already referred: 'That was the real concern, not so much what they had now but what they would have in the future, but that unfortunately was not expressed strongly in the dossier, because that takes away the case for war to a certain extent. But in the end it was just a flurry of activity and it was very difficult to get comments in because people at the top of the ladder did not want to hear some of the things … That's why there is an argument between the intelligence services and Cabinet Office/No. 10 because they picked upon it [the 45 minute claim] and once they've picked up on it you can't pull it back from them … the word-smithing is actually quite important. The intelligence community are a pretty cautious lot on the whole but once you get people presenting for public consumption then of course they use different words.' And indeed Tony Blair's foreword to the dossier includes the words 'The document published today is based, *in large part*, on the work of the Joint Intelligence Committee (JIC)'. (The emphasis is mine.)

So how did things stand in this first week of June? BBC journalists had put into the public arena accusations of the utmost seriousness about the conduct of government in a matter of national, indeed international importance. There was already great potential for embarrassment in that no progress had been made in discovering WMD in Iraq. Since Parliament and the nation had essentially been provided with a case for removing the threat posed by such weapons rather than a case for 'regime change' per se, this was an issue of enormous political sensitivity. Support for the war in Parliament had been by no means assured, and the publication of a frightening dossier, supported by the extraordinary parliamentary eloquence of Blair had been factors in securing it. If the Government had included in the dossier assertions about WMD knowing them at the time to be at best speculative and at worst untrue, utter disgrace would follow. Accusations of 'sexing up', of making mountains out of molehills whenever it appeared advantageous, were only marginally less serious. And of course a key element in the whole imbroglio was the 'Campbell factor'. Watching the programmes based on the published elements of his diaries (no doubt carefully chosen), improbably screened by the BBC, I gained a disturbing impression of an individual who had been badly in need of anger-management therapy while sitting at the right hand of the Prime Minister. In an administration notorious for 'spin' Campbell had been the supreme spin-meister. He was also a notorious bully, and well before the Gilligan affair he had regularly bombarded the BBC with grievances, complaints, criticisms and implicit threats.

In this environment the BBC had to be true to its principles; to withhold no well-founded criticism of activities involving any party including government which were demonstrably against the public interest. In a democracy, free media – in particular those associated with no particular political faction – have a cardinal role to play. It was interesting that in one of her broadcasts Susan Watts had mentioned the *Washington Post*, for it was the assiduity of that newspaper which had revealed wrongdoing at the very heart of the US government and ultimately brought down in disgrace the most powerful office-holder in the world. However, their investigative journalists had not been given carte blanche. Senior editorial staff had persistently emphasised to Woodward and Bernstein the distinction between reliable disclosure and rash speculation. We now had had assertions by BBC correspond-ents flatly denied by government up to the highest levels. Above all we had Alastair Campbell defending himself vigorously against an organi-sation he despised, attempting as he saw it to blacken his name. And certainly nothing could be more serious than to dispatch British soldiers to fight and die under false pretences. Either or both Government and BBC were now exposed to severe damage.

Two issues arise in considering the Hutton Report and its repercus-sions. I am conscious that some newspapers were quick to characterise the Report, with its absence of any severe criticism of government, as a 'whitewash'. For myself I approach this subject with a great deal of affection for, and loyalty to the BBC. My assessment of Alastair Campbell as an odious bully has not been altered by the publication of his carefully edited diary. Moreover I share the view that the war in Iraq has been a hideous mistake and that the support of Parliament in particular was in no small degree based upon unreliable intelligence. However, as an amateur historian I believe in going back to relevant sources. In this case there is rich and convincing material. Any reader can obtain on the web the full Hutton Report itself (not just the conclu-sions but extended passages of the evidence leading to them), and also the full roster of written and oral evidence including detailed exchanges between Government and BBC, and a later published article by Hutton justifying his approach and findings.

Was Hutton right to aim serious criticism at the BBC? Was he wrong in failing to aim such criticism at the conduct of Government? Would the outcome have been very different if the BBC had been vindicated, or even if it had shared criticism with Government?

It is now possible to trace in great detail the course of events following the Gilligan broadcast of 29th May 2003. The barrage began that very day with a communication from the Press Office at No. 10 to Mark Damazer of the BBC. The complaint was of the failure of the *Today* programme to contact Downing Street for a response to 'serious and untrue allegations about this office'. This use of words indicated that the specific reference to Campbell as having 'sexed up' the dossier would provoke a powerful personal as well as institutional response. The letter went on to complain that the BBC had continued to run the story in spite of a firm Downing Street denial, and pointed to the emphasis in BBC Guidelines on 'balanced reporting'.

This was the first salvo in an acrimonious exchange of correspondence between late May and late June. Some extracts will show the tenor and tone of the salvos from Campbell, who unsurprisingly emerged as the principal protagonist for Government. On 6th June, writing to Richard Sambrook, Head of News, he stated that 'all the intelligence in the September dossier was there with the complete authority of the JIC (Joint Intelligence Committee) … At no point has the reliability of Gilligan's source been questioned or discussed by the BBC … Do you have a process to filter out potential misinformation, gossip, unreliable or uncorroborated information? What is the process? In particular I would like to know what checks and balances have been applied to some of Mr. Gilligan's reporting of information from "anonymous sources" or indeed how the BBC's own Guidelines are applied. You cannot have missed the irony that one of the central (albeit false) charges against us (namely that the 45 minutes claim in the dossier was based on a single uncorroborated source) was itself broadcast on the word of a single uncorroborated source.' He went on to quote (accurately) from what he believed to be relevant provisions of the Guidelines: 'The authority of programmes can be undermined by the use of anonymous contributors whose status the audience cannot judge … contributors' credentials may need to be checked and corroborated several times. Documentary evidence may be needed to validate both stories and contributors' identities. It will usually be appropriate to seek corroboration from sources other than those suggested by the contributor.' After citing the Guidelines Campbell continued: 'You will, I imagine, seek to defend your reporting, as you always do. In this case you would be defending the indefensible. On the word of a single uncorroborated source, you have allowed one reporter to drive the BBC's coverage. We are left wondering why you have guidelines at all, given that they are so persistently breached without any comeback whatsoever.'

As the correspondence continued, Campbell's tone became increasingly demanding and belligerent. On 12th June he asked Sambrook '… will the BBC be conducting an internal inquiry into how one of its journalists could get it so wrong and be left unchallenged by his colleagues and bosses? … You have made very serious allegations which, if true, would amount to serious wrongdoing by me and my staff. Furthermore you have continued to repeat them with little reference to denials by the Chairman of the JIC and vindication by the ISC (Intelligence and Security Committee of the Commons).'

The assault reached a new level when Campbell wrote to Greg Dyke on 26th June: 'I am regularly assured by Richard Sambrook that when the BBC makes mistakes, you admit it. I'm afraid that is not the case and I have nine years of experience of this phenomenon … On the specific issue of the reporting of allegations about our and my conduct in relation to the WMD dossier, it has been a disgrace … I just ask you, as someone whose career and commitment I've always admired, to think about it. I am copying this letter to Gavyn Davies, and regard it as private.' On the same day Campbell wrote another tough letter to Sambrook, which was released to the press.

Before commenting on the more public exchanges between Campbell and the BBC, I wish to report and comment upon Sambrook's line of defence on behalf of the BBC.

Writing to Campbell on 11th June Sambrook could 'see no likelihood of us agreeing on this matter'. BBC journalism had not been driven by a single source. 'Andrew Gilligan has made it clear that one specific concern about the September dossier's presentation of the

Government's case derived from a single source. But the judgements that were made on the quality of the source and its usefulness were informed by a wider context. The fact is that a variety of sources, over a period of time, have indicated their concern about the way intelligence was used and presented in September ... Further, if we had thought the single source incredible we would not have reported the allegation at all ... We have not suggested that the 45 minute point was invented by anyone in Downing St. against the wishes of the intelligence community. We have suggested that there are pertinent and serious questions to be asked about the presentation of the intelligence material.'

On 16th June Sambrook sought to deal with the question of the application of the Guidelines. He wrote to Campbell: 'You continue to believe that Andrew Gilligan was in conflict with the Producer Guidelines. The Guidelines do say that our programme makers should be reluctant to rely on only one source. This guideline is not an outright ban, and I have explained in my previous letter Andrew Gilligan's judgement about that source (and the judgements of others involved in the decision to broadcast the story) were taken in context. A variety of sources over a period of time had spoken to BBC journalists about their concerns on matters relating to intelligence and WMD. However, we made it plain to the audience that concern about the dossier's presentation of the 45 minute WMD threat derived from a single source ... I should remind you that we have a Programme Complaints Unit which functions completely separately from presentation arms of the BBC such as BBC News and reports to the Director General with a right of appeal to the Governors. If you feel it would help, you could make a formal complaint to the Head of the PCU.'

Any prospect of reaching an understanding through exchanges of correspondence disappeared with the display of mutual acrimony and distrust which followed the developments of 26th June. In a letter of 27th June to Campbell, Sambrook made it clear that the attitude of BBC management had been influenced by earlier experience of dealing with Campbell. He wrote: 'It is our firm view that Number Ten has tried to intimidate the BBC in its reporting of events leading up to the war and during the course of the war itself'. He pointed to the affair of the discredited (and plagiarised) 'February dossier' as a basis for suspicion of a willingness to distort the facts. He emphasised that the allegations about the 45 minutes claim had been made not by the BBC but by its source. 'The BBC would have preferred it if the source had been on the record. But you will know that in this field sources rarely – if ever – choose to speak on the record.' While Sambrook volunteered that 'if the information provided by our source is *proved* to be incorrect we would make the fact very clearly known to our audiences and we would express regret. As we stand today that is simply not the case', he sustained a critical line in asserting: 'We have to believe that you are conducting a personal vendetta against a particular journalist whose reports on a number of occasions have caused you discomfort.'

Unsurprisingly this brought a robust reply from Campbell later that day. It proclaimed: 'The story was a lie. It is a lie. Every time the BBC continues its defence of the indefensible, it damages itself even more. I am a huge admirer of the BBC which is responsible for some of the finest journalists and journalism in the world. Their reputation is being undermined by its institutional failure ever to admit it is wrong.'

Such, then, was the public and private stance taken by the BBC during a critical month. Sambrook was, of course, a very senior and experienced journalist and manager. However the ultimate authority within the Corporation rested at management level with Greg Dyke, who as Director General was editor-in-chief, and ultimately with the Board of Governors chaired by Gavyn Davies and charged to protect the public interest.

It is, perhaps, surprising that by late June the Governors collectively had been given no opportunity to consider the denial by Government of what by any standards was a most serious and damaging allegation, and the wisdom of allowing that allegation to be broadcast and of continuing to defend it. In the evidence to Hutton we learned of an e-mail sent by Davies to fellow Governors on 29th June, following the bitter exchanges just described. He used these words: 'Some may … argue that there could be advantage for the BBC in reaching a settlement with No. 10 which both sides can live with, perhaps in advance of, or shortly after, the publication of the FAC [Foreign Affairs Committee] report. However, I remain firmly of the view that, in the big picture sense, it is absolutely critical for the BBC to emerge from this row without being seen to buckle in the face of Government pressure. If the BBC allows itself to be bullied by this sort of behaviour from No. 10, I believe that this could fatally damage the trust which the public places in us. Furthermore, I think we should remember that the main historic role of the Governors has been to shield the BBC from this sort of attempt to exert political muscle over our news output. This, it seems to me, really is a moment for the Governors to stand up and be counted.' Not surprisingly, this robust advice to Governors on a line to take before they had had a chance to examine staff, press for particulars or discuss the strengths and weaknesses of the BBC position came under examination by counsel at the Hutton Inquiry. Mr Sumption put it to Davies: 'You were so concerned about creating the outward appearance of succumbing to political pressure that you were urging the Governors that they should not give an inch whatever a further investigation of the facts might show'. In response Davies referred to 'absolutely unprecedented pressure from the Director of Communications at 10 Downing St.'

Of course Davies had discussed the matter with Dyke, and significantly with one of the Governors, Pauline Neville-Jones. She had been appointed during my time, and could bring to the Gilligan imbroglio the singular advantage of having been herself Chairman of the Joint Intelligence Committee. I had found her cold but formidable; Judi Dench as 'M'. There emerged a note from her to Davies which I found surprising. 'Gilligan reported a source as having claimed that the dossier was sexed up. We do not need to judge the accuracy of the source's claim and we have assurances from the Head of News that the source, though uncorroborated, was considered to be both reliable and in a position to know that it was right to rely on it.' In this setting Davies had delivered the dictum that 'the Board of the BBC cannot operate … unless it is in a situation in which it can rely on the good faith and competence of its officers.' This statement of absolute reliance on management was reinforced by another pronouncement in the evidence of Davies: 'The Governors are the Corporation of the BBC and the powers of the BBC bestowed by the Charter are bestowed on the Board of Governors. So it is the supreme authority of the BBC. I as

Chairman and my colleagues as Governors accept, therefore, our proper responsibility of the BBC in handling Mr Campbell's complaints ... We were acting as a supervisory authority, quite distinct, I think, from the activities of the management.' Yet Sambrook had held before Campbell the prospect of recourse to the Programme Complaints Unit, 'with a right of appeal to the Governors'. It can surely not be suggested that if the Governors had been required to act in that appellate role, their sole function would have been to assure themselves that senior managers were satisfied.

The Governors did not consider the issue collectively until their meeting of 6th July, almost two months after the initial broadcast. The statement issued at the conclusion of the meeting stated that the topic had been 'the allegations made by Alastair Campbell against the BBC's overall coverage of the Iraq War and the specific coverage of the September intelligence dossier by Andrew Gilligan on the *Today* programme'. Dyke and Sambrook had been questioned at the meeting. The statement totally denied Campbell's claim that large parts of the BBC had an agenda against the war. On the more specific issue 'the Board considers that the *Today* programme properly followed the BBC's Producer Guidelines in the handling of the Andrew Gilligan report which was broadcast on 29 May ... Although the Guidelines say that the BBC should be reluctant to broadcast stories based on a single source, and warn about the dangers of using anonymous sources, they clearly allow this to be done in exceptional circumstances. Stories based on senior intelligence sources are a case in point. Nevertheless, the Board considers that the *Today* programme should have kept a clearer account of its dealings with the MOD on this story and could have asked No. 10 Press Office for a response prior to broadcasting the story ... We are wholly satisfied that BBC journalists and their managers sought to maintain impartiality and accuracy during this episode.' In retrospect this statement begged a good many questions which were to be embarrassingly answered by Hutton. Was Gilligan's anonymous informant accurately classified as amongst 'senior intelligence sources'? Was it right to rely on a single anonymous source and make an exception from the general thrust of the Guidelines where the story was sensational in character and, if true, could end the careers of prominent people or even bring down the Government? How hard had senior management been pressed on the issues before Governors satisfied themselves of their assured 'impartiality and accuracy'?

In truth neither Gilligan nor Dyke himself emerged from cross-examination at the Hutton inquiry as fully deserving the Board's unqualified satisfaction. There continued to be some doubt as to how and by whom the name of Campbell had been introduced. Pointedly, in his ultimate report, Hutton would make a point of saying that he believed Watts and Hewitt to have been reliable witnesses; he chose not to characterise Gilligan in that way. There proved to be no less than three records of the meeting with Kelly. No contemporary record of the encounter recorded a direct accusation by Kelly that Campbell had sexed up the dossier by the insertion of a 45 minutes claim already known to be wrong. In relation to the allegation that the 45 minutes claim had not been inserted in the original draft of the dossier because it only came from one source, Gilligan in response to his own counsel had to admit this was wrong.

As for the behaviour of the editor-in-chief, there were grounds for believing that he did not appreciate early enough the gravity of the allegations against the Government in general and Campbell in particular. In evidence Dyke had to admit that 'I do not remember' whether by the time of Campbell's public attack on the BBC he had read the details of Gilligan's report of 29th May. 'Probably not ... I would,' he said, 'have received Stephen Whittle's account of the process.' He placed weight on a dubious argument. 'Oh, it is a pretty serious charge. But there is a distinction between a charge made by the BBC and a charge made by a source to the BBC.' He admitted that he had not seen, or sought to see, Gilligan's notes as a public response to Campbell's attack was being drafted. 'But we assumed that these replies were accurate.' Sambrook was to admit that 'I certainly think we should have paused and considered at greater length the charges that were being levelled against us.' Given the reliance, and I would argue the excessive reliance, by Gavyn Davies on the reliability of management, Dyke's casual attitude exposed the Corporation to the near certainty of grave embarrassment. At this time Dyke with his gregarious nature and empathy with creative and other staff was regarded within the BBC as a refreshing change from the rather Stalinist atmosphere of Birtism. I have to say, though, that in a crisis of the kind facing the BBC in 2003 the Governors in Birt's time could have been confident of rigorous scrutiny and meticulous examination of sources and records. The BBC was not a branch of show business, but an organisation seeking, and on the whole earning, the trust of the public. It was this degree of trust which blurred the distinction Dyke tried to make between an accusation made by the BBC and an accusation made to the BBC and broadcast by it. The general assumption would be that the BBC would give no credence to sensational allegations without being very sure of its ground. Claims heard on BBC Radio and voiced by a BBC journalist led to the conclusion amongst those who had grown to trust the integrity of BBC News and Current Affairs that 'It must be true. I heard it on the BBC.' A single source is particularly hazardous where he or she remains anonymous. If a hypothetical Kelly had come forward for interview he could have been asked whether or not he was part of the intelligence community, what precise part he had played in relation to the controversial dossier, and what grounds he had for suggesting improper intervention by No. 10 in general and Alastair Campbell in particular.

While the row between Government and the BBC was building up, the Foreign Affairs Committee of the House of Commons was conducting hearings on the claims about WMD. Appearing before them on 25th June, Campbell had used strong terms to say 'the story that I "sexed up" the dossier is untrue: the story that I "put pressure on the intelligence agencies" is untrue: the story that we somehow made more of the 45 minute command and control point than the intelligence agencies thought was suitable is untrue'.

On 7th July the FAC reported. Amongst its conclusions were the following: 'that the 45 minutes claim did not warrant the prominence given to it in the dossier, because it was based on intelligence from a single, uncorroborated source. We recommend that the Government explain why the claim was given such prominence ... that Alastair Campbell did not play any role in the inclusion of the 45 minutes claim ... that it was wrong for Alastair Campbell or any Special Adviser to have chaired a meeting on an intelligence matter, and we recommend that this practice cease ... that on the basis of the evidence available to us Alastair Campbell did not exert or seek to exert improper influence on the drafting of the September dossier ... that Andrew Gilligan's alleged contacts be thoroughly investigated.'

The subsequent reactions of the BBC and of Alastair Campbell showed that each party sought for a degree of comfort in these conclusions. Campbell said: 'I am very pleased that the FAC ... inquiry has found that the allegations made against me broadcast by the BBC are untrue ... I want to make it clear yet again that I fully respect the independence of the BBC ... Even now, all that I ask is that the BBC accept this, and I note that at no point did the BBC Governors in their statement last night claim that the story was true, merely that the BBC were within their rights to run it. This issue – the truth of the claims – is the only issue, and the one that the BBC should be addressing.'

The BBC, on the other hand, said it believed the FAC report 'justifies its decision to broadcast the *Today* programme story of 29 May and the *Newsnight* story of 2 June and shows that both were in the public interest ... It is because of BBC journalism that the problems surrounding the 45 minute claim have come to light and been given proper public attention. We note that the committee was deeply divided on the role Alastair Campbell played in the compilation of the September dossier and only reached a decision which supported his position on the casting vote of the Labour chairman ... We also note that not all the Labour MPs on the committee supported this decision.'

In truth a verdict in a political arena on the conduct of a controversial figure could hardly be regarded as a wholly detached judgement. Campbell had trodden on some self-important toes, and many elected members resented the reality that this appointee had more clout than most cabinet ministers. The wording on the question of 'improper influence' was guarded; not a denial of the possibility of such influence, but an absence of evidence 'available to us' to permit a definitive conclusion. The BBC were quite right in identifying concern about the insertion of the 45 minutes claim against the background of a total failure to discover WMD. Yet its justification shied away from the claim reported on the BBC that Campbell personally had been responsible for insertion of the 45 minutes claim to 'sex up' the dossier, even though it was known to be wrong. One could claim that consent for war had been obtained on the basis of information including at least one crucial element proved subsequently to be unreliable, but this was not the same as claiming deliberate manipulation and even falsification by a named individual. The FAC report was full of ironies. The BBC claimed to take comfort from it although it emphasised the vulnerability, in making the 45 minutes claim, of relying on a single source, just as Gilligan had done on the basis of his interview with Kelly. There was also a confusion as to what is or is not 'an intelligence matter'. Gilligan's broadcast gave the impression that his source, having been, he claimed, 'involved in preparing the Government's dossier' was himself a member of the intelligence community. In reality he had been a scientific expert and adviser on proliferation whose contribution to the dossier was limited and historical. The FAC expressed concern that Campbell should have chaired any meeting in the dossier context. As a civil servant of almost forty years experience I find it impossible to censure the involvement of the Director of Communications in preparation for the communication of complex matters to the public. The vital issue is the custody of the integrity of what is said. I was well used to meetings at which a Press Officer would say 'Would it not be clearer and more effective to put it this way?' And I might have to say: 'No. If you put it that way there is a risk of misleading.' In the case of the dossier, it has to be appreciated that the normal function of the JIC is to produce considered reports based on intelligence to a limited and privileged audience. The decision to expose the essence of the intelligence assessment to Parliament and the public made it sensible, indeed necessary, to deploy the skills and knowledge of experts in communication, but only in circumstances where the last word would rest with the intelligence community.

The controversy moved into a new phase with the admission by Kelly to his MOD managers that he had spoken to Gilligan, leading ultimately to the revelation of his name, his summons to a re-convened session of the FAC, and the tragedy of his suicide. On 9th July the Defence Secretary, Geoff Hoon, gave Kelly's name to the BBC, and described him as 'advisor to the Proliferation and Arms Control Secretariat in the MOD'. In response to this, Davies made it clear once again that the BBC would not reveal or confirm its sources.

When it was clear that Kelly would appear before the FAC, Gilligan took action which I would consider scandalously incompatible with the role of an impartial journalist. In an e-mail sent to an official of the Liberal Democratic Party he suggested questions to be put to Kelly which were passed on to a Lib Dem member of the committee. However, when Kelly gave his evidence the following day, 15th July, his evidence could not have given much comfort to Gilligan or the BBC. He made it clear that he had not been involved in reviewing drafts of the dossier, nor had he attended any meeting at which it had been discussed. He had simply prepared a section for inclusion, of which he said: 'It was not the intelligence component of the dossier, it was the history of the inspections, the concealment and deception by Iraq, which is not intelligence information'. Fed by questions proposed by Gilligan, a member asked whether the name of Campbell had come up in the exchanges with Gilligan. Kelly was rather vague. 'The Campbell word did come up, yes ... It came up in the conversation. We had a conversation about Iraq.' But in response to a direct question 'Do you believe that the document was transformed, the September dossier, by Alastair Campbell?', Kelly answered 'I do not believe that at all'.

I doubt very much whether, if there had not been the tragic development of the death of Dr Kelly, the dispute between Campbell and the BBC would ever have been subject to scrutiny at a public inquiry. As it was, every detail of the matter was probed in extensive cross-examination.

Hutton's conclusions were most damaging to the BBC. He found that 'the allegation that the Government ordered the dossier to be "sexed up" was unfounded'. He concluded that it had been wrong to suggest that Government 'probably knew the 45 minute claim was wrong' before it went into the dossier. The reason for the late inclusion of this claim was simply that the relevant intelligence report had come to hand late in the process. It was true that elements within the intelligence community would have favoured more cautious wording. In particular a Dr Jones had argued for this, but it had been a professional decision within the Joint Intelligence Committee to include the claim, although Jones would have preferred the term 'intelligence suggests' rather than the firmer wording 'we judge'. Evidence to the inquiry had made it clear that nothing would have been included against the advice of John Scarlett, chairman of the JIC. Hutton observed that there was nothing improper in the JIC considering suggestions from No. 10, although he conceded that Scarlett may have been influenced by the Prime Minister's known wish to make as strong a case as possible. However, there was no evidence of improper pressure or manipulation from Campbell. The inquiry unearthed records showing that Campbell had chaired a meeting at the Cabinet Office about preparation of the dossier on 5th September 2002 and followed it up in a memorandum to Scarlett. This had included the words: 'The first point is that this must be, and must be seen to be, the work of you and your team and that its credibility depends fundamentally upon that'. He said he was pleased to hear the intelligence community were 'going through the material you have. It goes without saying that there should be nothing published that you and they are not 100% happy with.' He added: 'I will chair a team that will go through the document from a presentational point of view, and make recommendations to you, and you can decide what you want to incorporate'. Presentational comments made did not include suggestions about the 45 minute claim, let alone suggestions made with the knowledge or suspicion that the claim was untrue.

Evidence submitted to, and probed by, Hutton made it clear beyond doubt that, on the basis of suggestions from a single uncorroborated source, the BBC had given credence to the most serious charge that support for war in Iraq had been obtained by reckless and dishonest means. They had stubbornly refused to retreat from their position, in spite of repeated denials from Government. After thorough consideration of all the material before the inquiry, I cannot fault Hutton's findings as they relate to the BBC.

Criticism, albeit more severe than expected, did not come as a total surprise to the BBC. Having regard, however, to the experience of the earlier 'dodgy dossier' and to the growing realisation that no WMD, let alone weapons capable of being activated in 45 minutes, would be discovered in Iraq, the Corporation had hoped for an 'everyone made mistakes' kind of report, after which the Government would prove to be the 'target of choice' for many media and other interests. They could retreat in good order under cover of a generous mea culpa and a promise to learn from the experience. So why did Hutton not pursue matters into areas likely to embarrass the Government? From those cheated of their quarry came frankly insulting suggestions that Hutton had been chosen as a judge likely to be cautious and discreet, so as to assure Government of a comfortable whitewash. It was noteworthy that until publication of the report, there had been pretty universal acclaim for Hutton's conduct of the inquiry; for his courtesy, openness and thoroughness. I wonder how many of those who subsequently pilloried the report took the care to read, as I have done, every single word of the proceedings and evidence. Hutton had no favours to seek; as a Law Lord he had reached the height of his profession. As an Ulsterman he was more detached than most from mainline politics. And to sit on the Bench through the worst days of 'the Troubles' required no lack of moral or physical courage.

In the report itself Hutton reflected on his interpretation of his terms of reference. 'The major controversy which arose following Mr. Andrew Gilligan's broadcasts on the *Today* programme on 29 May 2003 and which closely involved Dr. Kelly arose from the allegations in the broadcasts (1) that the Government probably knew, before it decided to put it in its dossier of 24 September 2002, that the statement was wrong that the Iraqi military were able to deploy weapons of mass destruction within 45 minutes of a decision to do so and (2) that Downing St. ordered the dossier to be sexed up. It was these allegations attacking the integrity of the Government which drew Dr. Kelly into the controversy about the broadcasts and which I consider I should examine under my terms of reference. The issue whether, if approved by the Joint Intelligence Committee and believed by the Government to be reliable, the intelligence contained in the dossier was nevertheless unreliable is a separate issue which I consider does not fall within my terms of reference.'

A wider inquiry into the justification for the Iraq War would have taken much longer and inevitably much evidence would have had to be heard in confidence. Hutton wanted an inquiry seen to be conducted in the open. As a jurist, I believe he was what American jurisprudence terms a 'strict constructionist'. He would not stretch his terms of reference to take in a much wider series of issues than the circumstances surrounding the sad death of Dr Kelly. That task would fall later to Robin Butler and his Privy Counsellor colleagues. It should never be forgotten that, while the BBC suffered serious institutional damage which impacted on the careers of some protagonists, those who lost most in the entire affair were the family of Dr Kelly, a man who had 'done the state some service' and been plunged into terminal despair by the consequences of a single indiscreet contact.

However, the consequences of the Hutton Report for the BBC were profound. In spite of his conviction that the report was one-sided, Gavyn Davies took the view that as a man of honour he must resign from the chairmanship. This was a very great pity. He was a person of great experience and deep knowledge of the workings of the BBC. One could argue that he had taken too far the principle of reliance on senior management. He had discouraged the Board from conducting anything resembling an independent probe. But press and public opinion remained very divided, and Davies could have weathered the storm, rather than leaving the Corporation under caretaker arrangements at a critical time.

On the other hand, Greg Dyke had no thought of resigning and regarded the decision of the Governors that he should leave as supine. His reactions are recorded in his self-revelatory book *Inside Story*. Frankly it reeks of cocky arrogance and a displeasing element of class animosity. His contempt for the Board of Governors and the whole system of governance shines through, and I find it revealing that he goes out of his way to admit he classified Sarah Hogg and Pauline Neville-Jones as 'the posh ladies'. Yet his enforced departure produced from BBC staff across the country an extraordinary outpouring of affection and regret. After the austerities of the Birt regime, the informal and unstuffy approach of Dyke had cheered people up. He was not a slave to management consultants but concentrated on the programmes and programme-makers. After the Birtist winter, they felt cherished. One could say that Dyke had wonderful credentials to manage any broadcaster other than the BBC. However, I say again that the BBC was not just another broadcaster. At the core of its mission and reputation lay the reliable, honest and impartial coverage of news and current affairs, with the necessary corollary of a willingness to admit the inevitable mistake made by individuals in a complex organisation. In the evidence presented to Hutton, Dyke had shown a lack of a sense of urgency and real meticulous thoroughness in investigating a most serious complaint.

I fear that in this unhappy episode the BBC in general and Dyke in particular reacted to a sense of being under siege from Campbell, not just in relation to the Gilligan broadcast but over the longer term. The earlier episode of the 'dodgy dossier' and the evident failure to unearth WMD in Iraq created a general feeling that Government could not be trusted on the Iraq issue. Internal BBC documents disclosed at the inquiry, such as the e-mail sent by Davies to the Governors, reveal a state of mind that the pressure from Government would have to be resisted to preserve the independence of the Corporation, rather than that the merits of specific criticism should be addressed with an open mind. Let me recall the fear I had expressed at the time of Dyke's appointment. I had worried about his overt Labour sympathies and connections, not because they would lead him to favour Labour, but because he might have to lean over backwards to avoid any appearance of weakness under Government pressure. And of course at that time I had no idea that he would find himself in double harness with a chairman from the same camp. I am sure Dyke did not rationalise his reaction in this way, but I would regard it as a relevant factor in the debacle alongside his failure to take sufficiently seriously his responsibilities as editor-in-chief of the most trusted and prestigious news organisation in the world.

At a stroke, then, the BBC lost both its Chairman and Director General, leaving the unfortunate Vice Chairman, Lord Ryder, to eat the inevitable humble pie, and the Deputy Director General, the admirable Mark Byford, to steady the ship of management. While the eventual choice of Mark Thompson as Dyke's successor brought a most able professional back to the BBC after a relatively short stint at Channel 4, I am convinced that his exposure to this damaging interregnum damaged Byford's chance of winning the crown. In due course Michael Grade would be appointed to be the last chairman of the BBC Governors. This was not a good appointment. Grade's very great talents lie in the broadcasting component of show business, and are essentially executive in character. Having led the BBC in arguing for a reasonably generous licence fee, Grade would 'jump ship' to become Executive Chairman of its principal competitor. I saw in this nothing of the dedication to the distinctive role of the BBC for which I would look in its most senior positions.

Two other significant developments would follow, and Government would no doubt assure us that their decisions were not influenced in the slightest by the fallout of the Hutton Report. The historic basis of BBC governance was fundamentally changed under the new Royal Charter of 2006. At the end of that year the Board of Governors would be replaced by a BBC Trust, which would be distanced from management and would be concerned with 'setting the overall strategic direction of the BBC including its priorities, and … exercising a general oversight of the work of the Executive Board'. It had been anticipated that Grade would move from chairmanship of the Board to chairman-ship of the Trust, but his unexpected defection left Chitra Bharucha, as Vice Chairman of the Trust (and an old colleague at the Northern Ireland Broadcasting Council) holding the fort until the appointment of Sir Michael Lyons. The other piece of the reorganisational jigsaw was the formation of an Executive Board, replacing the old Board of Management and adding to nine senior BBC executives (with Thompson in the chair), five non-executive members led by Marcus Agius of Barclays and with backgrounds in business, communications and the law. Were these changes in the interest of the BBC and the public, and why did they occur at this time? In an earlier chapter I have explained why I felt the existing pattern of governance, with constant formal and informal interaction between the professionals and those charged to protect the public interest, was better than the then hypo-thetical alternatives. I would not change that view. But the case for retention of the Board was diminished by the over-passive role played by the Governors in the Gilligan affair, and Dyke himself who regarded the Governors with a degree of contempt had no doubt made those views known outside the BBC. It could well be the case that Grade, while supporting the change in principle, did not look forward to the more nebulous role of Trust Chairman, and that this was a factor in his move to a full-blooded executive position at ITV where, as Executive

Chairman, he would be monarch of all he surveyed. The BBC also found itself faced with a licence fee settlement which would leave it unable to pursue some of its ambitious plans but would on the contrary require economies and retrenchment.

10

A CLOUDED FUTURE

I have, I hope, made clear in the foregoing how much the BBC has been a valued part of my life, not just as one privileged to serve two terms as a Governor but as one of the many who admired its standards and values, enjoyed its programmes, and used it as window and mirror to enlarge my knowledge and experience. I continue to wish the Corporation well in the future, but in these closing reflections I have to acknowledge dangers and failings, as well as triumphs and opportunities.

What was a virtual monopoly for a powerful radio-based medium when the wonderful and impossible John Reith took the helm of the infant Company and Corporation, has become over time only one player – albeit a powerful and prestigious one – in a very crowded market-place of communications. The technological change and development presented to us not so long ago as futuristic visions have become current realities. The simple radio receiving sound or television receiving sound and pictures have been supplemented by a huge range of ever more versatile devices; the boundaries between camera, telephone, receiver and transmitter of sound, vision or text have completely broken down. These irreversible realities have inevitable implications for broadcasting and its funding. Potential income derived from licences permitting use of conventional radio and television sets will be at risk in a future where a growing number of consumers will look elsewhere and use other technologies for most or all of their information or entertainment.

Then we have also to reckon with the extraordinary proliferation of broadcast sound and television channels. I vividly recall Patricia

Hodgson, not so very long ago, explaining to Governors the hand-held device which would allow us to choose or switch channels in the digital future. I recall John Birt, who kept in touch with the leading-edge American technological gurus and was far-sighted about the emerging digital future, discussing with us the opportunity to 'save' programmes, to use material earlier transmitted live as a vast library of sound, vision and text, allowing the enthusiast to call up (say) all the Cup Finals contested by Liverpool or Manchester United since the matches were recorded. By the end of 2007 the BBC had announced the launch of the iPlayer allowing the owner to access programmes up to 7 days after transmission or up to 30 if downloaded.

That future is our present. Every evening Elizabeth and I have available to us a huge number of radio and television channels, courtesy of a Sky package. They range from the 'heavy hitters' of BBC, Sky, ITV or CNN to tacky little low-cost programmes appealing (one assumes) to fanatic minorities who can never have enough of porn, or golf, or cooking, or interior decorating, or whatever turns them on. Sport and movies are huge audience lures. If one wants to be sure of access to top-class rugby football or soccer, Grand Slam tennis or 'Majors' golf (as I myself do) it is necessary to pay a Sky subscription. Of course certain sports occasions have always been regarded as 'great national events', as part of the cultural fabric which holds the country together, and this has motivated limited Government action to ensure free-to-air availability on BBC or ITV. The attractiveness of televised sport has had a marked effect on sport itself as well as on broadcasting. Those who hold the rights to sporting events and are aware of their potential value are quite unsentimental about breaking long-established and hitherto harmonious relationships with the BBC or others. In turn the purchasers of rights exert great influence on the scheduling and timing of events. A great sport like rugby football, previously played by all and still played by most for fun, becomes at the highest levels increasingly corrupted by money, while the flow of funds from rights and other sources pushes the rewards for elite soccer players to levels bordering on the obscene.

The inevitable consequence of exponential channel prolifera-tion is a gradual reduction in the hours spent by the average viewer or listener in hearing or watching BBC programmes. It has, by and large, remained gratifyingly the case that the BBC remains the broadcaster of choice to which viewers turn for great royal or national occasions. It continues to attract huge audiences at Christmas. There are still few indeed who do not tap into BBC services to some extent. Nevertheless, the average audience size and the average number of hours viewed per week on BBC channels have fallen and will inevitably continue to fall. Moreover it is falling because so many viewers, while continuing to pay the obligatory licence fee which supports the BBC, have opted to pay in addition the subscriptions necessary to access competitive channels. It is hardly surprising, then, that those who pay significant sums for digital packages, and subsequently use the subscription channels for the bulk of their viewing, increasingly resent paying as well a licence fee to fund programmes they access less and less.

The technological challenge is exacerbated by a generational challenge. It is a platitude to say that the young generation are the listeners and viewers of the future; but platitudes, however boring, are frequently true. I have described how, in my own case, listening to BBC Radio was a fact of life in the 1930s. We did not have to be weaned off something else to digest the BBC; we had tasted little else. Today young people cannot bear to be separated from music, whether at home or outside it. In a trance-like state, like so many nodding dogs, they walk our streets oblivious to anything but the 'portable' music available to them. As for vision, it seems that a great number prefer 'games', preferably with a great deal of simulated mayhem, to the more didactic character of mainline TV channels.

BBC's inevitably contracting audience is today served by a proliferating range of channels and programmes. On television, digital technology affords access to BBC3 and BBC4 as well as News 24 and BBC World; the BBC Radio of my infant days now transmits on Radios 1, 2, 3, 4 and Five Live, as well as a host of local stations (such as Radio Ulster and Radio Foyle in Northern Ireland). Now we also have diverse digital radio offerings such as Radio 7 for children, Radio 6 for cutting-edge new music, the BBC Asian Network and others. The future of both radio and television will be a digital one. There is a real challenge in furnishing all these outlets with programme material consistent with

BBC aspirations. The use of 'repeats' on BBC1 or BBC2 is a subject of frequent criticism; but if one looks at the schedules of BBC3 and BBC4 the reliance on 'repeats' is strikingly obvious. One can dress all of this up in the language of 'an opportunity to see again' or 'a chance to see something you missed first time round', but there is a legitimate question as to how useful it is for the BBC to proliferate rather than concentrate. There may, too, be a risk of encouraging the broadcasters to be timorous; to confine something fine, but novel and testing, to a minority channel before exposing it to the broad audience of the mainline channels.

I return to a central dilemma. Although many efforts have been made to do so, no one to my mind has produced a credible alternative to the licence fee as a means to ensure for the BBC a high degree of independence and stability. The capacity to form taste rather than slavishly to follow it is due in no small measure to the freedom to break the crude bonds of the market. Complete recourse to subscription could, over time, develop an approach and a mind set indistinguishable from other broadcasters. Recourse to advertising would represent a real threat to the financial stability of ITV.

Yet, as I have acknowledged, the licence fee basis does not afford a compete shelter from government pressure or influence. In setting its forward level, governments are bound to reflect any wider public sentiment that the BBC is too extravagant, too ambitious and imposes on the viewing and listening public costs disproportionate to the perceived benefit. It can, of course, also import into licence fee decisions some element of judgement of the BBC's past performance and conduct, and I suspect this played a part – regardless of Government disavowals – in the most recent relatively stringent settlement following the Hutton Report. The plain fact of the matter is that the licence fee settlement fell short by some £2bn of the funding sought by the BBC to carry it forward to 2013. As a consequence, BBC income from the licence fee over this period will fall short of keeping step with anticipated inflation. To cope with this situation, the initial reaction of management was to seek savings of 2.7 per cent per annum, but this target was increased to 3 per cent by decision of the Trust. Against this background, substantial redundancies were proposed, with the inevitable adverse reactions from staff. By March 2008 BBC Resources would be sold off, while the iconic TV Centre would be disposed of in 2013. By that year television production would have been reduced by 10 per cent, and to the great surprise of many, including the present author, those 'factual' programmes regarded by many as jewels in the crown would take a particularly severe 'hit'. The renowned Natural History Unit in Bristol would lose a third of its programme-makers. Real fears were being voiced within the Corporation about the future of the in-house documentary. Substantial television production would move to centres outside London. There would be a consolidated newsroom in London for television, audio and online.

So the future over the next six years is at best challenging. This is not to say that previous efforts had purged the BBC of all duplication and extravagance. In the nature of things, the licence fee pitch to government will always be in terms of forecast disaster if not met in full. Then, if the outcome falls far short of both desires and expectations, management will speak confidently of a leaner but more efficient business. In reality, management and the Trust face the daunting task of servicing a range of radio and television outlets much more numerous than when I joined the Board in 1991, while coping with an ongoing media revolution (including the digital switchover and the re-engineering of web services) within a finite resource. The challenge will be to preserve the BBC as a powerful creative entity, as distinct from a multimedia publisher. There are great opportunities in the area of multiplatform production, affording the same quality of experience on the web as viewers expect on their television receiver.

However, licence fee funding is at least assured for a further period. What will happen at the end of the current settlement is much less clear. Will the government of the day be willing to persist with a licence fee at all? By then, more and more people will be accessing entertainment and information through other channels than a television receiving set. The share of viewing and listening time devoted to BBC programmes will have fallen further. Even if there is a future licence fee, will it continue to be used solely to fund the BBC? The Conservative Party are already canvassing the idea of a fund to support 'public service broadcasting', however provided. If a 'tax on reception' is no longer feasible, could public service broadcasting, whether provided by the BBC alone or by others as well, be funded out of general taxation? What would this mean in terms of freedom from excessive government influence? If the BBC were to be faced with a much reduced income from licence fee or an equivalent, would it fall back on defining and maintaining its core purposes, either abandoning other activities or seeking other modes of funding such as subscription or advertising? I was impressed by an attempt by Phil Harding, in an article in *Ariel* for 2nd October 2007, to define these core purposes as 'political independence, accuracy and fairness, a sense of proportion and perspective'. In the same article he urged the Trust to move beyond the role of regulator and remind everyone 'what the BBC is there for'.

That is indeed a basic question: what is the BBC for? What is unique and distinctive about it that should, in the wider national interest, be preserved in all circumstances? It may seem trivial, but I would argue that not the least of the benefits offered by an independent BBC is the availability of high quality programmes unpunctuated by advertising breaks. In my account of interviews in America in the 1960s, I have recalled with amusement the experience of trying to explain serious issues amidst constant interruptions to trumpet the virtues of dietary drinks or improbably efficient detergents. There would be uproar at the National Theatre or the Royal Opera House if acts of *Hamlet* or *Tosca* were to be interleaved with advocacy for heterogeneous consumer products.

On radio, there is an interesting comparison between Radio 3 and Classic FM. I have already confessed, in discussing the contribution made to the BBC by Liz Forgan, to being tuned in to Classic FM as I drive my car from point to point. I can tolerate in that context the endless repetition of the same 'classics', the transmission of 'snippets' rather than complete and extensive orchestral works, interspersed with crass advertising exhorting me to hire a personal injury solicitor or protect myself against the consequences of cracks in my windscreen. I can even endure the endless cheery 'matiness' of many of the station's presenters. I do not want to be grudging; what it seeks to do it does very well and it clearly serves the tastes of a very substantial audience. The appearances of David Mellor remind me of what we lost in terms of a minister with a real cultural hinterland. But Classic FM does not offer, nor can I see any competitor offering, what is available on and through Radio 3: the uninterrupted transmission of serious and lengthy compositions, both familiar and unfamiliar, the regular broadcasting of live orchestral music from the BBC Proms or elsewhere, and the total or substantial support of indispensable high quality orchestras. In my native Northern Ireland, for instance, the BBC is not the sole funder of the Ulster Orchestra, but without its support, coupled with the performance of its music on local and network BBC programmes, any prospect of maintaining that orchestra would disappear.

I have described how, as I joined the Board in the early 1990s, Birt and others generated a fundamental debate about the BBC's future positioning in the broadcasting marketplace. The option of Himalayan elitism was rejected, and the case was made for a continuing BBC presence over an enormous range of topics and genres, but aspiring always to be excellent in its own right. I had, at the time, much sympathy with this line of argument, but I now begin to wonder how tenable it will prove to be over the long term. While I would think it ridiculous to turn up one's nose at BBC participation in a 'war of soaps' (Will *Eastenders* challenge *Coronation Street* for the Championship? Will *Emmerdale* win promotion to the Senior League?), one asks from time to time how far audience-chasing is compatible with the pursuit of excellence. I must say that, if the 'soaps' are truly a window into modern Britain, the picture they present is at times a depressing one. In a country now notorious throughout Europe for the drunken hooliganism of its citizens while 'enjoying themselves', we are presented with a fictional world in which most meetings take place in a pub, and where producers desperate for novelty and striking pre-publicity offer us an unappetising diet of rape, murder, incest, drug addiction, sexual infidelity and other fare to titillate the jaded palate of the viewer.

All of this is in the context of a depressing social coarsening. Of course the old high-falutin' 'BBC English' sounds ridiculous to modern ears, as Prime Ministers or members of the royal family shy away from anything 'posh' and adopt the safe tones of 'Mockney'. As someone who grew up with an Ulster accent, the son of an audibly Mancunian mother and a father raised in Cardiff, I rejoice in the relaxed exposure to national audiences of our diversity of genuine regional speech. I have, of course, my personal likes and dislikes. Try as I may, I cannot find great linguistic charm in unadulterated 'Brummie', even when spoken by as excellent a Board colleague as Bill Jordan; if there had been more trade union leaders like him, we would be a better Britain today. So I make no plea for a universal accent. What I do profoundly object to is the increasingly slipshod use of our magnificent language, without regard to structure or grammar or pronunciation. In particular, programmes aimed at children and young people are too often presented by attractive and vivacious youthful presenters with great charm and liveliness, but no feeling whatever for the language in which they speak. Yet if our nation has one immeasurable treasure, it is the fact that it is the home and origin of a great world language, which we share with the English-speaking world and offer as a lingua franca to people everywhere.

I am, though, concerned about more than the use of our language in contemporary broadcasting (and, indeed, in contemporary society). I identify a disturbing incidence of cloning and cruelty. Too much broadcasting has become repetitively formulaic. Someone, somewhere, has a bright idea. Let's see how well complete novices in a particular activity cope with ballroom dancing, ice-skating, singing, juggling or whatever. And in no time 'the industry' adopts with enthusiasm a whole new format for 'audience participation' shows. More disturbing is the underlying element of cruelty in some examples of this genre. BBC was not, thank goodness, responsible for the crass *Big Brother*, although the current Director General, Mark Thompson, came back to the BBC from its progenitor, Channel 4. It is, in my view, morally little better than a 'freak show' in Victorian London. If the Elephant Man were alive today, he would probably be offered a place 'in the House'. One accumulates a disagreeable collection of sleazy misfits, throws them together, eavesdrops on unedifying encounters, and exposes the viewer to exchanges of conversation plumbing new depths of banal idiocy. Occasionally some person hitherto deemed reasonably sane accepts a role in the show, presumably on the mistaken assumption that all publicity is good publicity. I cannot recall any scene more demeaning to our politics than the sight of a Member of Parliament – a man of strange views but of formidable articulacy and intelligence – behaving like a total idiot in a ridiculous costume. Yet this was a man who had run rings round a patronising committee of the US Senate, so that I for one had admired his chutzpah while detesting his opinions.

While the BBC avoids many of the worst excesses of programmes like *Big Brother*, it does present Anne Robinson in *The Weakest Link*. As I have mentioned earlier, Robinson in my time as a Governor had chaired a public meeting in Derry with marked charm and intelligence. It has been a great financial success for her to re-invent herself as the cruel dominatrix of *The Weakest Link*, but is it really wholesome entertainment to witness contestants taunted, humiliated and dismissed? It may be said that contestants know what they are letting themselves in for, and that in any case it is 'only a game'. It is unhappily the case that many people seem prepared to accept any humiliation to enjoy the Warholian five minutes of fame, but should we be encouraging this Gadarene submission to self-abasement?

I have a special concern about the exposure of young children to humiliation and disappointment. It is supposedly great fun for an audience to prolong suspense, to allow the camera to linger on the faces of young contestants as the 'result' is deliberately delayed, but too often I have seen quite young children leave a competition with dismay and disappointment etched on their features. We are, of course, told that children welcome and embrace the competition, and realise and accept that they may not succeed. But is this always so; or is it rather the case that stupid parents push them into these situations? I think of the Chinese father who is apparently entirely happy to encourage his very young daughter to run hundreds of miles a week in the hope of future athletic success, regardless of its possible impact on her long-term health.

Another area of growing concern is the manipulation of an audience; inducing them to incur telephone costs in contests they cannot win; presenting staged events as spontaneous; misrepresenting the nature of a programme. It was a great shock to confidence in BBC standards when shadows were cast over such flagship programmes as *Blue Peter* or *Children in Need*. This manipulation is certainly not unique to the BBC; indeed it is probably less of a feature there than elsewhere.

But because the BBC is party to an implicit compact with its listeners and viewers involving trust, an episode such as the misrepresentation of the Queen's photographic session with Annie Leibovitz was peculiarly damaging. It was sad that Peter Fincham, a most talented individual, thought it right to resign, but the affair was an 'own goal' of embarrassing magnitude. Of course the entire relationship of the BBC with the Palace is a complex one. For many years the public looked to the BBC as the sole or prime broadcaster of great royal occasions: coronations, State Openings, Trooping the Colour, royal weddings and funerals. The designation of a Royal Correspondent of great experience reflected the Corporation's determination to recognise and respect the position and functions of the Head of State. Inevitably the Martin Bashir interview with Diana, Princess of Wales, did not enhance that relationship. It was revealing to hear the Prince of Wales, interviewed on the Alpine slopes alongside his sons, muttering under his breath, but all too audibly, words of dislike and contempt for Nick Witchell, in my own experience one of the nicest and most professional of BBC correspondents.

Are BBC standards really slipping; and if so, why? One must expect an error of judgement or worse on the part of the Corporation to receive much more extensive coverage in the other media than similar incidents identified at other broadcasters. This reality reflects both the general expectation of higher standards from the BBC and the disposition of media empires with broadcasting arms to take every opportunity to discredit a formidable competitor. The BBC is not some impersonal machine but a human organism with inevitable weaknesses as well as strengths; its standards are the standards of those who work in and for it. Of course any organisation of human beings will, in the nature of things, sometimes be guilty of human error, no matter how admirable its guidelines and standards. I have consistently taken the view, since long before I became associated with the BBC, that the best shield for the Corporation's independence is a readiness to confess to error wherever and whenever it occurs; we should resile from the doctrine of infallibility but reflect on the benefits and virtues of confession. Unfortunately the saga of the Gilligan/Kelly affair is not the only occasion on which a frank admission and apology, far from harming the BBC, would have limited damage to it.

I believe, however, that developments in the Corporation and the industry have made the BBC over time more vulnerable. For much of its existence, those recruited to the BBC looked upon it as beginning a long-term commitment to the Corporation and its ethos. It was comparable with joining the Diplomatic Service or the 'Indian Civil'. In those early years the Corporation was in any case the sole British outlet for such talents, but in time the emergence of independent programme companies offered to ambitious and talented people the prospect of employment elsewhere in broadcasting, and sometimes for more attractive pay and conditions. For many years the BBC retained something of the character of a rather strange government department, including an addiction to bureaucracy and the designation of managers by the initial letters of their post description rather than by their surname or even (unthinkably) their first name. This atmosphere must at times have been suffocating, particularly when the strange and ascetic Reith was in command, yet many of these earlier generations of long-term BBC staff regarded themselves as 'guardians of the sacred flame' and privileged to work in an organisation of high ideals and in a building proclaiming 'Nation shall speak peace unto nation'.

I was not too late a comer to miss contact with people who had been totally committed to the BBC as more than 'just another broadcaster'. I think of colleagues and friends like Michael Checkland, who joined the BBC as a Senior Cost Accountant at 28 and left it as Director General at 56; David Hatch, who was a producer for BBC Radio at 25 and left as Advisor to the Director General at 54; John Tusa, who became a BBC general trainee at 24 and left as Managing Director of the World Service at 56; Will Wyatt, a sub-editor of BBC Radio News at 23, who left as Chief Executive of BBC Broadcast at 57. These were BBC men through and through. By comparison John Birt spent some thirteen years of a thirty-two year career in broadcasting at the BBC, and I believe his record shows someone full of energy and ideas yet in some way never quite in tune with the fundamental ethos of the Corporation. And as his successor we had Greg Dyke, whose short term of four years at the BBC followed a diverse and distinguished broadcasting career with TVam, TVS, LWT, GMTV, Channel 4, B

Sky B, and Pearson. A splendid career; but was it, I wonder, the best preparation for leading the world's greatest public serving broadcasting organisation to spend so many years in organisations committed to the profit motive and the provision of acceptable entertainment?

I do not for a moment seek to argue that the senior positions at the BBC should be reserved for a kind of enclosed priestly class. Yet it is a fact that twenty years have passed since the Corporation last appointed a Director General from the ranks of long-service BBC staff, although Mark Thompson returned to base after a relatively short stint at Channel 4. Overall, I fear that a rising percentage of BBC staff look upon the Corporation as 'just another broadcaster'. In a sense Birt's misjudgement in seeking to remain as Director General a contracted manager rather than a member of the permanent BBC staff indicated a certain lack of total commitment to the employing Corporation.

None of this would have mattered as much but for the trend towards 'out-sourcing'. There are analogies here with many other areas of public activity. I myself, like many others, had served for a time on a Hospital Trust, in our case responsible for three local hospitals. The idea of freeing the hospitals to concentrate on things only they could do – diagnosis and treatment by surgical, medical or nursing care – by contracting out seemingly peripheral activities, sometimes described loosely as 'hotel services', such as catering, cleaning and security, initially seemed both logical and attractive. Companies whose main business was the cleaning of hospitals and other premises would, it was assumed, make a better job of it than in-house staff. In practice it was all too often the case that the previous in-house staff carried on with their old jobs under a new employer but with much less favourable conditions. An activity embodied in a caring service was re-embodied in a company inevitably driven by the profit motive. In the reorganised health service managers proliferated but responsibility became diffuse. The old-fashioned matron, mocked in 'Doctor' films and elsewhere, disappeared and there was no longer that all-powerful ward controller using staff directly responsible to her to ensure cleanliness and efficiency. Small wonder that we have MRSA!

When I joined the Board of the BBC in 1991, the Corporation remained a fascinating and comprehensive complex of transmission, production and publishing experience. A Director of Engineering, Bill Dennay, served on the Corporation's Board of Management and oversaw the maintenance of the extensive BBC transmission system. An efficient and reliable system was fundamental to broadcasting. However bitterly some listeners and viewers might complain about programmes not to their taste, this was as nothing compared to the outrage of licence payers whose reception of sound and/or vision was unsatisfactory. They were impatient of explanations that in some areas reception was affected by the topography. They became cross if there was 'down time' in reception as transmission facilities were overhauled. But early in my term the Corporation was obliged to dispose of its transmission facilities.

Historically the BBC had maintained a large and diverse programme production capability. My first visit to the Television Centre had been organised by my cousin John Bloomfield, costume designer for *The Six Wives of Henry VIII*, and I had seen then the huge volume of costumes and properties as well as the extensive studio facilities. But the BBC came under constant pressure for suppressing, by allegedly unfair competition, an independent production sector of great vigour and with huge growth potential. Bowing to this argument, Government imposed upon the BBC a requirement to 'buy in' 30 per cent of its programme output from independents.

Those of us who go to the movies or watch films at home are well used to seeing on the screen some such rubric as 'A Daniel Goldstein picture, made by Megalomania Productions for Hyperbole Films'. So, too, we have become more and more used to seeing on our television screen, at the conclusion of some programme, whether commissioned from London or through other centres (including BBC Northern Ireland) a reminder that it has actually been made by some independent production house. The externally-imposed requirement to meet a quota of independent production was followed, after a report by David Hatch already referred to, by an internal commitment to work to a quota of programmes commissioned from BBC centres outside London. In the event, considerable numbers of programmes would count towards both quotas, as having been commissioned from independents by centres outside London.

Superimposed upon these changes we have the withdrawal of the BBC from its self-reliance on internal 'resources'. So in time even a production made for network at the Television Centre could well bring together freelance actors or performers with independent resource providers, who would work equally happily for the BBC or any commercial production centre. Just as George III's armies were reinforced with Hessians, and 'British' soccer or rugby teams now draw on players from around the world, so the old 'regular army' of the BBC has been reinforced by organisations of mercenaries, for whom a BBC project is no different from a project undertaken for any other broadcaster. It is significant that the controversial Queen versus Annie Leibovitz film was commissioned from an independent. Who, then, should bear responsibility for the foolish and embarrassing misrepresentation of the Queen's behaviour? For myself, I feel strongly that the more BBC activity is 'out-housed', the greater is the emphasis which should be placed by commissioners on quality control, in the widest sense of that term.

I hope I am not being merely sentimental when I write how deeply I regret the replacement of the BBC Governors by the BBC Trust. It is not irrelevant here that in his memoir *Inside Story* Greg Dyke displays a remarkable degree of arrogant contempt for the Governors with whom he worked. 'I have,' he writes, 'never been one to respect position for its own sake and I was hardly likely to start in my fifties, particularly when dealing with a group of people most of whom knew absolutely nothing about the media, and who would have struggled to get a senior job at the BBC … I was not a fan of the system and made that obvious at times.' It is clear that during his time he preferred to deal man to man with Gavyn Davies and ignore other Governors as much as possible. I hope I have shown in the previous chapter the appalling dangers in such an approach. Dyke wanted to get rid of the Governors, and the Governors, in too readily and uncritically accepting his advice, probably facilitated their own replacement. For myself, the role of the Trust reminds me of an anecdote, probably apocryphal, from Winston Churchill's final years in Parliament. 'Who's that?', he inquired testily, as an MP unknown to him rose to speak. 'Bossom, sir'. 'Bossom? Bossom?', said the great man. 'Neither one thing nor the other.' But I must not rush to judgement. The Trust must be judged on its performance.

In my mid-term London University seminar I had sought to address the merits of the existing system of governance compared with the idea of 'the Board across the street'. Frankly I felt that a regular interaction between the two Boards (of Governors and Management), each realistic about the ambit of its own responsibilities, would serve the Corporation better than a more remote and detached supervisory Board or Trust. I felt that, in his evidence to Hutton, Davies had over-stressed the supervisory nature of the existing Board of Governors and understated its ultimate responsibility and authority.

Dyke's criticisms would be offensive were they not so ridiculous. Governors were not chosen, and should never have been chosen, as suitable to win 'a senior job at the BBC'. They were chosen to ensure that a great public corporation, enjoying the enormous privilege and advantage of an assured income, held to the highest standards of integrity, impartiality and independence. However I felt a degree of vicarious pride when, on the precipitate resignation of Michael Grade, one of my former BCNI colleagues, Chitra Bharucha, as deputy designate to Grade, became on an acting basis Chairman of the BBC. Our numbers had thus produced a President of Ireland and a Chairman of the BBC. I await the succession of others to the See of Canterbury or the Apostolic throne!

I foresee extremely testing times ahead for the BBC, particularly if incidents of evasion, misrepresentation or dubious integrity were to recur. I see a very real danger of the BBC becoming less and less an 'author' and more and more of a 'publisher', drawing upon the creative talents of outside agencies. I suspect that the Corporation has already spread itself too thinly, with its multiple radio and television channels and its far-sighted exploitation of the internet. If I had to choose between maintaining the present broad scope and reach, while relying increasingly on sources of funding such as advertising or spon-sorship, and a narrower scope still largely funded by a licence fee at a level deemed defensible in a developing and enormously competitive market, I would opt for the more selective approach if required to protect the BBC's traditional independence. It does not take any great talent to buy in Hollywood movies or popular American sit-coms. The first priority of the BBC should be to do surpassingly well things which others cannot or will not do.

At the heart of the BBC's mission I would place the gathering and transmission of truthful, unbiased and carefully presented news and the production and transmission of current affairs programmes which help to build a more thoughtful and participatory democracy. I often reflect how ludicrous it is, at a time when old-fashioned meetings are a thing of the past, that the broadcasting parameters for General Elections are so tightly drawn. In America, contenders for consideration within the principal parties appear together to be judged by the primary electors, while the chosen presidential candidates will go head to head before a vast television audience. The control-freaks of British politics are so far unwilling to take that risk. Alongside mainline domestic News and Current Affairs, I would emphasise the importance to the BBC, the nation and the world of maintaining the highest standards in the World Service and BBC World, and of using a great documentary tradition to explain and illuminate complex issues.

Inside the UK the BBC has many critics, not all of them disinterested; outside it has a vast army of admirers. If Britain still enjoys a degree of respect in many countries around the world, in spite of post-colonial resentment and our involvement in problematic military adventures, it is in no small degree due to the BBC's world-wide reputation for seeking to tell the truth without fear or favour. Again and again on visits abroad, foreigners have told me that they give no credence to their state-owned or state-controlled broadcaster's coverage of events in their own country. The Voice of America came to be seen long ago as an instrument of US foreign policy, and even the commercial American broadcasters find it hard to shed a kind of cultural jingoism. American coverage of an Olympic Games can sometimes give the impression that only Americans are competing. In India, on the other hand, as quintessential an Englishman as Mark Tully nevertheless conveyed the impression of his absorption by, and love of, all things Indian. It is, of course, an anomaly that the FCO money is available only to fund the radio-based World Service. While there are still areas of the world beyond the reach of television and reliant for news on primitive radio sets, there are huge television audiences in areas of the world now developing very rapidly, in many of which there is a great hunger for an improved grasp of the English language.

By 'documentary' I mean programmes capable of getting below the surface of complex issues, and making the arguments clear and credible to mass audiences. This can be a tricky area. In principle the BBC does not have a 'position' on any of the great issues of the day. Yet it has to be acknowledged that, by and large, those who work in the creative front-line trenches of the BBC do not in every respect reflect the profile of the population as a whole. Strenuous efforts have been made, and not without some heartening success, to close gaps of gender and race. Indeed I sometimes worry that the portrayal of 'multicultural Britain' has become almost too formulaic and prescriptive, in that televised fictional hospitals always feature black consultants, courts of law black QCs and police forces black superintendents. I wonder from time to time if those 'represented' in this way do not feel vaguely patronised. However, some recent analysis suggests that the BBC attracts more than its share of what the outspoken Lord Cocks was wont to call 'the chattering classes'; the *Guardian*-reading, down with Israel, perdition to Bush section of society. The need for 'balance' is proclaimed and in principle accepted throughout the BBC; but there is a danger of a reluctance or failure to challenge 'views held by all right-thinking people'. And it is in any case ridiculous to suggest that every pro must be offset by a matching con. To insist upon 'balance' in each individual programme would be absurd and unworkable. As I have argued earlier, a programme about some development in medical or other science does not have to give equal weight (whatever equal weight is) to counter-views asserted only by a tiny minority. Professor Dawkins does not need to be given a disclaimer after every religious broadcast, but there must be a room in schedules for the expression of his acerbic scepticism.

There are and will be some real and important challenges in the balanced explanation of complex issues and arguments. For some years it remained possible, in theory if not in practice, that the British people would be asked by referendum to endorse or reject a proposal to join the Euro-zone and abandon the pound sterling. In such a referendum, citizens would be asked to reach a judgement on issues of great technical complexity. The BBC above all would have had a responsibility to rise above the inevitable crude political sloganeering, to allow the case for or against to be made fully, using all the artifice of media professionalism to illuminate and explain the great issues at stake. Global warming; the rise of militant Islam; the economic ascent of India and China; the threat of AIDS in Africa and elsewhere: these great issues of the day and many others need and deserve honest, thorough and unbiased exposure to the British people.

No one can excel the BBC in its presentation of the wonders of natural history, of travel to strange and exotic places, of the great cultures and monuments of the past. No one can better help us to understand recent history. The televised exploration of the dismemberment of Jugoslavia, *The Death of Jugoslavia* was an object lesson in clear-minded analysis. The BBC can take us around our coastline, up our mountains, into castles and gardens and great houses. It can give us a sense of who we are and where we came from; our ancestry and even our DNA.

Of course this ambitious mission cannot be carried to completion solely on the basis of documentary material. Fiction also has a powerful part to play. Here, though, we do run into the strength in the creative community of a particular political and moral view of the world. Most, though not of course all, of the contemporary writers of drama for transmission are from a distinctive liberal camp with a fairly predictable approach to many issues. Oddly enough I share with Ken Loach the distinction of being an Honorary Fellow of our mutual old college, St Peter's at Oxford, and I greatly admire his cinematic skills so rightly acknowledged by his peers at Cannes. Yet it was entirely predictable that his fine film *The Wind that shakes the Barley* should bathe Irish 'freedom fighters' in a golden glow as they contested the iron fist of brutal British militarism. In my own prolonged experience of Ireland – North and South – brutes, idiots and martyrs are more evenly distributed between competing factions. While I join a multitude in thinking Margaret Thatcher stayed too long and went too far, I look in vain at most drama set in her reign for any recognition of the previous excesses of trade union barons prepared to hold government and country to ransom.

News, current affairs, documentaries, voyages of exploration in time and place: these should in any circumstance be cherished and protected as centres of excellence. Drama by instalments earns a place in schedules; but must the BBC follow other 'soaps' ever more rapidly down-market, into long-running freak shows? *Our Friends in the North* showed that there is high drama and wonderful entertainment in recreating dramatically situations which illuminate the true life of our nation at different times in its recent history.

It is desirable to inform and educate young people as well as to entertain them, but not to patronise them with crass contemporary chatter. It would be no loss to our civilisation to drop ridiculous game shows, absurd contests for amateurish talent or pathetic fame-seekers, and all programmes verging on the cruel or capitalising on the vanity of foolish or deviant people.

We must never forget that the origins of the BBC lie in radio, not in television. When the family at the end of a long day looks for entertainment or information, it is more likely than not to turn to the TV set. Yet for much of the day sound is much more accessible than vision. Here BBC still has much to offer which is truly distinctive. Radio 3 is unique, and a major underpinning for classical music. Radio 4 continues to transmit programmes of unique authority which often shape the political debate of the day. Radio 5 Live is important because, in a nation passionate about sport, it builds and maintains contact with younger listeners.

But if, in a pressurised and increasingly competitive future, the BBC had to consider unpalatable measures of retrenchment, questions may have to be asked about the distinctiveness of Radios 1 and 2. Radio 1 distinguishes itself from commercial competitors in the genre of popular contemporary music by its dedication to transmitting from live concerts and its popular outreach events around the country. Radio 2 attracts a large audience to 'easy listening', offering an agreeable and popular mixture of music and enjoyable chat (at which Wogan is the master). Yet, in my heart of hearts, I am not fully convinced that these stations occupy cultural space which would otherwise be empty. Pop songs and amiable conversation would not be despoliated by advertising breaks, and there are other broadcasters fully capable of serving these particular audiences, particularly in the age of digital radio. Radio 2 has been Britain's most popular radio station, but I am not convinced that its offering would suffer if not funded through a licence fee. Yet if the BBC were to move to a 'mixed economy', confining programmes funded from a restricted licence fee to those meeting a more stringent 'public interest' test, while moving to a subscription or advertising basis for more populist albeit popular output, one could envisage an uproar from the existing commercial sector at the prospect of the BBC consuming a share of its cake. Clearly the BBC Executive Board and Trust appreciate the need to apply themselves to the challenge represented by tighter licence fee funding and the need for a further 3 per cent efficiency saving per year between now and 2012. Mark Thompson was quoted by *Ariel* in July 2007 as commenting: 'There are only three ways of bridging the gap. We can increase our planned efficiencies over the next few years, cross some new investments off the list, or switch funds from existing commitments to new ones'. The third of these options is of critical importance. The BBC cannot stand still as technology and the market change; it must continue to innovate, and a willingness to venture the new may require the review and pruning of the familiar. Again, to quote Thompson, 'If we want a BBC which still has great ambitions and values, a BBC which is still an indispensable part of the life of this country and of hundreds of millions of people around the globe, we've got to transform virtually every part of it'. In a graphic phrase, he described his position as Director General as 'being like carrying a Ming vase while simultaneously roller-skating down a flight of stairs'.

If broadcasting is changing, so too is the nation, the United Kingdom of Great Britain and Northern Ireland. During my eight years as a Governor one of the most tricky issues we faced was that of the 'Scottish Six'. Some years ago in my native province, the ineffable Gerry Adams favoured us with the thought that 'they [the IRA] haven't gone away you know'. Nor has the issue raised in Scotland. In a radically changing UK the tension between the classic view of a unitary state and the current reality of devolution now in force in Scotland, Wales and Northern Ireland was bound to surface sooner or later. Since Scotland was the standard-bearer for 'regional nationalism'

last time round, it is hardly surprising that a Scottish National Party
First Minister in Alex Salmond had returned to the issue. On the earlier
occasion the central issue was the continuing Anglocentricity of the
national news bulletin, often dominated by news of Westminster developments with no bearing on Scotland's affairs. Greg Dyke had once
characterised the BBC as 'hideously white'; Salmond nimbly characterised it as 'hideously White City'. However the potential agenda reaches
well beyond the single issue of a 'Scottish Six'. Salmond rightly sees the
BBC as an enormous cultural patron, but one which sucks talent away
to London and undervalues and underuses the capacity in Scotland and
other regions to serve the network from a local base. Modern Scotland
clearly feels itself to be 'a nation once again', albeit not yet the independent one Salmond and the SNP wish it to be. If Scotland had as large a
cohort of Gaelic speakers as Wales has of Welsh speakers, there might
well have been a Scots counterpart of Newyddion long ago.

I confess to some fear of a progressive erosion of the BBC's independence of government. This has never been absolute, given government control of charter and licence fee. Yet before I left the Board,
I found myself as chairman of the Audit Committee accompanying
Christopher Bland to brief Chris Smith on the annual report. Now
we see pressures to regard the Corporation as simply another public
body, to be subject to the full rigorous processes of the Comptroller
and Auditor General and Public Accounts Committee. To the politicians this may seem entirely appropriate, given the heavy reliance of the
Corporation on public funding. From long experience as an Accounting
Officer in government, I can testify that subjection to these processes
leads to a risk-averse mentality, and fear of risk in a creative community
can have a most stultifying effect.

With all its problems, challenges and occasional human failure,
the BBC remains to this day a unique and uniquely valuable institution. Towards the end of my second term as a Governor, the Canadian
Broadcasting Corporation (CBC) suggested that a BBC Governor
should attend its annual board conference for 1999 to be held that year
at Mont Tremblant in Quebec (in winter a ski resort). Christopher Bland
nominated me to take up this invitation. My encounter with the CBC
board underlined the variety and diversity of that vast country. Sitting

at dinner on my first night, I could not fail to notice the pronounced Irish brogue in the speech of my neighbour at table. 'When did you leave Ireland?', I innocently asked. 'Sure, I was never in Ireland at all.' He was from Newfoundland. I do not know what, if anything, they learned from me, but what I learned from them was their respect, admiration and envy for the BBC: its reputation, scope, funding and independence. Everywhere I have travelled in the world (and I have been in many countries inside and outside Europe) I have found the same thing. It was, therefore, an enormous privilege to have been, for eight fascinating years, 'one twelfth of the Corporation', to serve alongside colleagues of the calibre of Baroness James, Sir Richard Eyre and Norman Drummond, and interact with such dedicated professional broadcasters as Bob Phillis, Will Wyatt or Ron Neil.

In 2007, having published a book, *A Tragedy of Errors: The Government and Misgovernment of Northern Ireland,* I was invited to speak at the literary festival in Wigtown, the Scottish equivalent of Hay-on-Wye. One of the other speakers on the day I was asked to perform was Marista Leishman, daughter of John Reith and mother of Mark, to whom I have referred earlier in this book. She had written an unsparing account of his unpleasant and domineering relationships with his family. He seems to have been essentially a bitter and twisted man, never offered in his life after the BBC any position he deemed an adequate acknowledgement of his greatness. Perhaps it took a ruthless and austere megalomaniac to cherish and nurture the dream of a new medium offering to all knowledge and entertainment, speech and drama and music.

His portrait and bust still brood over the Council Chamber at Broadcasting House. He fought for the infant BBC as if it were the family he should have cherished as well or better. Wherever his troubled soul now resides, of this at least he can be proud.

Index